The War for Spiritual Battles

The War for Spiritual Battles

Identifying Satan's Strategies

Bill Vincent

© 2016 by Bill Vincent.

All rights reserved. No part of this book may be reproduced, stored in a retrieval system or transmitted in any form or by any means without the prior written permission of the publishers, except by a reviewer who may quote brief passages in a review to be printed in a newspaper, magazine or journal.

All Scripture quotations are from the Authorized King James Version of the Bible unless otherwise noted.

Softcover 978-1-60796-542-8

Hardcover 978-1-304-74527-9

PUBLISHED BY REVIVAL WAVES OF GLORY BOOKS & PUBLISHING

www.revivalwavesofgloryministries.com

Litchfield, IL

Printed in the United States of America

Table of Contents

Chapter One APPRAISAL OF THE BATTLEFIELD 7

Chapter Two THE GREATEST WARFARE EVER KNOWN 13

Chapter Three SATAN'S MOTIVATION 21

Chapter Four CAN A CHRISTIAN BE DEMON POSSESSED? 35

Chapter Five COULD A DEMON BE CONTROLLING YOUR LIFE? 45

Chapter Six GOD'S ARMOR AGAINST SATAN'S ATTACK 57

Chapter Seven LOCATING THE ENEMY 71

Chapter Eight SATAN'S FIELD OF ACTIVITY 86

Chapter Nine THE FATHER'S GLORY 94

Chapter Ten THE INVISIBLE WAR FOR YOUR MIND 114

About the Author 124

Recommended Books 126

Chapter One
APPRAISAL OF THE BATTLEFIELD

We will begin by taking a real look at the battlefield. Many times for us to win battles, we need to understand all aspects of the field of each and every battle.

- Terrorism continues to run rampant on a worldwide basis as confirmed by the daily news broadcasts.

- More babies have been killed in America during the past years than people murdered in all of history's wars!

- An average of 2,260 babies are aborted daily here in the United States.

- Approximately 58,200 children are abducted each year in the United States.

- More than one million young people are sexually molested, filmed, or photographed in the United States for child abusers or for the thriving "kiddie porn" trade.

- In 9 out of 10 cases of child sexual abuse, the abuser is a family member or someone close to the child.
- Since 1980, the number of unwed mothers has jumped 250 percent. Illegitimate births among teenagers jumped from 199,350 in 1970 to 394,370 in 2007.
- One out of every fifteen high school students smoke pot almost daily. The average beginning age of children drinking alcohol is 14 years of age.
- Today nearly half of all marriages end in divorce. About one third of all U.S. families are single-parent families.

These are just a few of the terrible conditions of which we are aware. Every day our newspapers carry similar or worse information. Optimists claim that "things" are going to get better, but are they? And, if so, when?

Listen to what the Word of God says:

2 Timothy 3:13 But evil men and seducers shall wax worse and worse, deceiving, and being deceived.

2 Timothy 3:1-4 This know also, that in the last days perilous times shall come. For men shall be lovers of their own selves, covetous, boasters, proud, blasphemers, disobedient to parents, unthankful, unholy, Without natural affection,

trucebreakers, false accusers, incontinent, fierce, despisers of those that are good, Traitors, heady, highminded, lovers of pleasures more than lovers of God;

It is also a sad fact that under the status quo of the past several years, heathen ways has far outstripped the church world.

During the first 200 years after the death, resurrection, and ascension of Jesus, the disciples had reached the whole known world with the influence of Christianity. Almost the whole world was Christian by some definition. Contrast that with the statistics of our day. Although the World Almanac lists 23 percent of the world's population as Christian, their figures include every denomination — Catholic and Protestant — as well as many cults who use the name of Christ, but deny His power and His teachings. It is estimated by many Christian organizations that less than six percent of the world has truly been discipled for Jesus.

With the population continuing to explode in heathen countries, we have reached almost a zero population growth in North America due to birth control, "living together" arrangements, increasing homosexual liaisons, and legalized abortions.

It is estimated that every year over 80 million people are added to the world's population—unsaved, unreached people. When we look at the rise of lawlessness in North America and the escalating population of non-Christian and Christian nations, the task before the real Church of Jesus Christ is formidable. Must we withdraw from the arena of life, overwhelmed at what the forces of evil are doing, paralyzed by the weight of population statistics and the desperate needs we see in people's lives?

Not at all. There is an answer. We, as God's children, as His called, chosen, and anointed, are that answer. Jesus said, *"Ye are the light of the world..."* (Matthew 5:14).

God's Word also tells us:
1 John 4:4 Ye are of God, little children, and have overcome them: because greater is he that is in you, than he that is in the world.

Romans 8:37 Nay, in all these things we are more than conquerors through him that loved us.

God means for us to have victory—total victory! He means for us to take the world for Jesus Christ. It can be done. It must be done. We can do it! However, in order for us to do it, something must happen—it must happen in us!

The Church and the individual Christian have a greater challenge today than at any time in history. In God's dealing with Israel and in the history of the Church, the point of greatest crisis brought forth the greatest manifestations of the power of God.

Man had to seek God for it. It did not come automatically! When Israel began to pray and to seek the face of God, a revelation came that restored the power, that restored the vitality to the spiritual life of the individual and the nation—but man had to seek it. Man must sincerely desire to know and possess this power in order to receive it.

God's answers are not always easy to accept. Sometimes they demand tremendous dedication of our lives. One of the greatest secrets I have learned through times of great trial and decision is to always trust the Holy Spirit. What may at the moment appear difficult may be the very doorway into the most beautiful experience and blessing of your life.

You are approaching such a doorway right now. Do not be afraid to step through it. Victory and power in every area of your life awaits you on the other side.

We have made a spiritual breakthrough which is the revelation of our time. The early Church, which took almost the entire known world for Christ, had this outlook:

1. They recognized the existence of evil spirits.

2. They knew that evil spirits deceived and possessed men.

3. They understood that the devil was out to hurt, kill, and destroy humankind.

4. They knew that Christ gave His followers authority over them through His name!

5. They recognized their enemy—not things, not surface results.

6. They located their enemy.

The Church of Jesus Christ today, as in the days of its beginning, must lay hold on the spiritual equipment of the apostolic period for dealing with the influx of the evil if it is to take our world for Jesus Christ. This is what the revelation of the New Anointing is all about.

Chapter Two
THE GREATEST WARFARE EVER KNOWN

The Holy Spirit wants us to understand the real warfare we all are facing every day.

What is the most horrible war or atrocity that your mind can visualize?

Was it the Civil War when hundreds of thousands of mere teenagers were pressed into service; where they were forced to serve under famine conditions with unspeakable sanitation and scant medical attention, with thousands killed, maimed, or scarred for life?

Was it the great conflict known as World War I where more advanced technology resulted in the ability to kill more people in a shorter period of time and again left thousands dead or mutilated?

Perhaps you think of the senseless and bloody political purgings such as Vietnam, Uganda, or other dictatorial countries. Your mind may picture with terror some war yet to come, perhaps a nuclear exchange which will wipe out man completely and devastate the earth as depicted in science fiction literature and films.

Bible scholars may think immediately of the record in the Book of Revelation when blood will flow as high as the horses' bridles, or the 39th chapter of Ezekiel which prophesies of those who will be killed and left to be eaten by ravenous birds and beasts of the field.

All war is terrible beyond description—short ones as well as long and bloody ones—but none mentioned, nor indeed any war which ever has been or ever will be, can equal in scope, violence, or catastrophic results the war which has been going on for thousands of years and has claimed millions upon millions of victims—men and women, boys and girls. A war which has destroyed lives, homes, fortunes, health, minds. .which has hurt, killed, tormented, and enslaved. .which has spared neither infant nor elderly. .which has seen no quarter given, but has been and will continue to be a war to the very end of time.

The war of which I am speaking is not a war of swords or guns. It is not a war of armed might or nuclear potential. It is a war that embraces all humankind that does not spare a single person, small or great. It literally, personally, and vitally involves every soul that is ever born into this world without a single exception. This warfare has existed from the beginning of time and can be documented back to the Garden of Eden. It lies at the base of all wars which have ever been fought, all conflicts, all strife, all disasters, whether involving mighty nations or individuals.

It is the war between the only two opposing forces that there are or ever have been in the existence of the world—God and Satan, good and evil. While this warfare has resulted in very real material damage and physical carnage, its roots are neither in the material, nor the physical realm. It is a spiritual battle. It is a battle which pits men one against another, husband against wife, daughter against mother, brother against brother, sister against sister. But the real warfare is and always has been Satan against God, God against Satan.

Many men through the ages, including theologians of great renown, have denied the existence of a real devil, yet the proof of his existence is everywhere. The results of his work are indisputable. Hiding the reality of his existence is one of the cruelest hoaxes he has ever perpetrated on men.

But not all are deceived. Many great men of God have seen his work and testify to his reality. Billy Graham had this to say: "All of us engaged in Christian work are constantly aware of the fact that we have to do battle with supernatural forces and powers. The devil follows me every day.... He tempts me. He is a very real presence to me."

He also declared: "There is a connection between the devil and the increase of drugs, pornography, sexual license, and the occult in the U.S. We see people who are committing all kinds of violence, mass murders, and we have learned they have been involved with the occult. The very word 'witchcraft' stems from the same Greek word as the word 'drugs.'"

Pope Paul VI declared: "The smoke of Satan has entered the temple of God through a fissure in the church. ...Evil is not merely a lack of something, but an effective agent, a living, spiritual being, a terrible reality, mysterious and frightening."

Evan Roberts, the great Welsh revivalist, said: "The devil's great purpose, for which he fights, is to keep the world in ignorance of himself, his ways, and his colleagues; and the Church is taking sides with him when siding with ignorance about him."

The Bible itself clearly teaches that Satan is an entity, a being, a real personage:

Ephesians 6:11, 12 Put on the whole armour of God, that ye may be able to stand against the wiles of the devil. For we wrestle not against flesh and blood, but against principalities, against powers, against the rulers of the darkness of this world, against spiritual wickedness in high places.

The thief [Satan] *cometh not, but for to steal, and to kill, and to destroy...* (John 10:10).

Neither give place to the devil (Ephesians 4:27).

2 Timothy 2:26 And that they may recover themselves out of the snare of the devil, who are taken captive by him at his will.

Revelations 20:1, 2 And I saw an angel come down from heaven, having the key of the bottomless pit and a great chain in his hand. And he laid hold on the dragon, that old serpent, which is the Devil, and Satan, and bound him a thousand years,

Even men who are not known for their religious bent have taken note of the reasons behind the great struggle manifested in the world between nations and ideologies. They see that the real battle of this world is not between countries or ideologies.

"Any of our contemporaries readily identifies two world powers, each of them already capable of entirely destroying the other," he declared. He pointed out, however, that understanding of the split often is limited to a political conception and to the illusion that danger could be abolished through successful diplomatic negotiations or a balance of armed might.

The fight for our planet, physical and spiritual, a fight of cosmic proportions, is not a vague matter of the future; it has already started. The forces of Evil have begun their decisive offensive, you can feel their pressure....

A nation must stand for something of spiritual and not only material value, and the key to the decline of the spirit is in religion. Spokesmen from every walk of life realize that something is going on behind the scenes of nations that far outweighs what can be seen with the natural eye. They can only conjecture what may lie ahead.

We are geared to think of many different forces at work in the world—the United States and Russia, Israel and the Arab countries, communism and democracy, battles for key governments, conflicts caused by powerful money or oil interests, the cry for "human rights" coming from many factions and groups. The world is a battleground for many conflicts.

The entire picture, however, boils down to the fact that there are only two forces at work in the world. When we realize that, and when we realize what these two forces are—what they stem from, what their thrust is, what is at stake—we will understand that unless something happens, this world is on a collision course that not only will destroy the world, but will plunge countless millions of men and women, boys and girls into the hopeless torture of an eternal hell.

The world today very definitely is on a collision course, not with other worlds but within itself, and no man-made ark can offer the solution. A far from cheerful picture is set forth in this chapter, but it is a necessary picture. Unless we get the true focus of what is really going on behind the scenes, we never will know what we are combating, much less how to combat it.

The scene is set—God against Satan, good against evil, righteousness against sin. The world is on a collision course, and millions of people will be affected from their homes (families) to their jobs, physically, mentally, spiritually. Does this affect you? And what can we, as children of God, do about it?

Chapter Three
SATAN'S MOTIVATION

Understanding satan's motivation is revealing the secrets behind it all. As violent as the warfare between good and evil has been, and as long as it has been going on, it is not eternal. God has no beginning of days nor ending. He is from everlasting to everlasting. That is not true of Satan. God is eternal. Satan is not. God is the great I AM—ever existent. Not only was He in the beginning, He was before the beginning. He made the beginning. He is the beginning, and He will continue to exist eternally without end!

Satan did have a beginning, and there will come a time when he will meet his just end. His beginning was as a heavenly being created by God—not as the bearded caricature we often see pictured by artists, but as a glorious creature of magnificence in the Heavenlies. His name at that time was Lucifer, which literally means "light-bearer." Isaiah refers to him as Lucifer, son of the morning.

Ezekiel carries this description of Lucifer's former glory:

Ezekiel 28:12-15 Son of man, take up a lamentation upon the king of Tyrus, and say unto him, Thus saith the Lord GOD; Thou sealest up the sum, full of wisdom, and perfect in beauty. Thou hast been in Eden the garden of God; every precious stone *was* thy covering, the sardius, topaz, and the diamond, the beryl, the onyx, and the jasper, the sapphire, the emerald, and the carbuncle, and gold: the workmanship of thy tabrets and of thy pipes was prepared in thee in the day that thou wast created. Thou *art* the anointed cherub that covereth; and I have set thee *so:* thou wast upon the holy mountain of God; thou hast walked up and down in the midst of the stones of fire. Thou *wast* perfect in thy ways from the day that thou wast created, till iniquity was found in thee.

Because of Lucifer's pride, self-exaltation, and rebellion, he came under God's judgment and was cast out of heaven. These events also were described by Ezekiel:

Ezekiel 28:16, 17 By the multitude of thy merchandise they have filled the midst of thee with violence, and thou hast sinned: therefore I will cast thee as profane out of the mountain of God: and I will destroy thee, O covering cherub, from the midst of the stones of fire. Thine heart was lifted up because of thy beauty, thou hast corrupted thy wisdom by reason of thy brightness: I will cast thee to the ground, I will lay thee before kings, that they may behold thee.

The event was also recorded by Isaiah who gave further details of Lucifer's transgression:

Isaiah 14:12-14 How art thou fallen from heaven, O Lucifer, son of the morning! *how* art thou cut down to the ground, which didst weaken the nations! For thou hast said in thine heart, I will ascend into heaven, I will exalt my throne above the stars of God: I will sit also upon the mount of the congregation, in the sides of the north: I will ascend above the heights of the clouds; I will be like the most High.

Impressed with his own beauty and high rank as the "cherub that covereth," Lucifer became obsessed with the desire to usurp God's throne, take over heaven, and himself become the object of worship. He was severely judged by God for this rebellion with the assurance of far greater punishment to come. However, Lucifer never lost his burning desire to be worshiped. From that desire and Satan's hatred of God stems all the havoc which has taken its ugly toll in the lives of people down through the ages. Lucifer (now known as "Satan," the "devil," "adversary," etc.), in seeking to achieve dominion in heaven, led a rebellion among the angels, recruiting vast numbers of them for his own purposes. This rebellion was put down by God and Satan was cast out of heaven.

Everyone has seen the caricatures which depict Satan with pointed ears and tail, dressed in a red suit, with a wicked gleam in his eye and a pitchfork in his hand.

Ephesians 6:12 For we wrestle not against flesh and blood, but against principalities, against powers, against the rulers of the darkness of this world, against spiritual wickedness in high *places.*

We confront not only Satan, but hordes of principalities and powers. Evil spirits come against us to seek our destruction by causing us to disobey God and His commandments and walk in the flesh, thereby robbing the Spirit.

Many people wrongfully suppose that when God cast Lucifer out of heaven, he gave Satan the world for his domain. That is not so, for we read in Genesis that God gave dominion of this earth to man, who was His crowning creation. In the six days of creation described in Genesis 1 and 2, God brought forth a perfect creation on this earth through His creative Word.

On the first day, He said, "Let there be light" and there was light. On the second day, He made the firmaments of the heavens. On the third day, God said:

Genesis 1:9 And God said, Let the waters under the heaven be gathered together unto one place, and let the dry *land* appear: and it was so.

When God looked over what His Word had performed to that point, we read: *"...God saw that it was good"* (Genesis 1:10). God continued with further work on that third day, and it was again noted that *"it was good"* (verse 12).

On the fourth day when God created the luminaries (sun, moon, and stars) and on the fifth day when He created the fowls of the air, fish of the sea, and the beast and cattle of this earth, each time it is noted: *"...God saw that it was good"* (Genesis 1:18, 21). Then came the creation of man.

Genesis 1:26, 27 And God said, Let us make man in our image, after our likeness: and let them have dominion over the fish of the sea, and over the fowl of the air, and over the cattle, and over all the earth, and over every creeping thing that creepeth upon the earth. So God created man in his *own* image, in the image of God created he him; male and female created he them.

This act took place on the sixth day. When God looked back over what he had done on that particular day, it was not just "good" as other days had been, but we read that *"...behold, it was very good"* (Genesis 1:31). The creation of the sixth day was viewed with a great deal more satisfaction than the preceding five days had been, not just because of the creation of man, but because God announced His great plan for blessing humankind.

Genesis 1:28-31 And God blessed them, and God said unto them, Be fruitful, and multiply, and replenish the earth, and subdue it: and have dominion over the fish of the sea, and over the fowl of the air, and over every living thing that moveth upon the earth. And God said, Behold, I have given you every herb bearing seed, which *is* upon the face of all the earth, and every tree, in the which *is* the fruit of a tree yielding seed; to you it shall be for meat. And to every beast of the earth, and to every fowl of the air, and to every thing that creepeth upon the earth, wherein *there is* life, *I have given* every green herb for meat: and it was so. And God saw every thing that he had made, and, behold, *it was* very good. And the evening and the morning were the sixth day.

Besides man himself, God included something else very important in that day's satisfactory creation. He included his plan for man. God blessed man. That was part of his plan. He told man to be fruitful, multiply, and replenish the earth. That was part of His plan.

God gave man dominion over everything He had made on earth—over the fish of the sea, the fowl of the air, over every living thing that moved on the earth. He also gave him the bounty of the plentiful food supply brought forth by the vegetation.

God gave man dominion. That was His plan for man. This dominion is a very integral, very vital part of that day's creation and is the very root of the study we have undertaken on spiritual warfare.

God gave man dominion. This creation over which God gave man dominion is more fully described in Chapter two of Genesis, which describes the Garden of Eden God planted and gave to man as his natural habitat.

You can see how this rejects the theory held by many Christians that when God cast Satan out of heaven, He sent Satan down to earth and made him the prince or god of this world. Nothing could be further from the truth. God gave man dominion over this world and everything that is in it. He gave into Adam's hands the keys of dominion of this earth.

One has only to read today's headlines, listen to the heartaches of people, or just see the condition of people on the streets to know that this is not the situation as it exists today. It is easy to see that, instead of having dominion, man is under dominion. You can see from the open wickedness of the land, from the cruel tragedies which are a daily occurrence that man is not in control. He is under bondage, in slavery to forces outside himself.

You can see from people's lives and from hearing their heartaches that Satan has taken the dominion away from man and is usurping the great blessings that God intended for man to have. Why? What has happened? Why isn't man using the keys of dominion he was given? Because he gave them away. Adam took the keys of dominion that God gave to him and he handed them over to Satan.

Along with the blessings that God gave man in the Garden of Eden, along with the duty of dressing and keeping the garden, along with dominion over every living thing, God gave man one more very important thing. He gave him responsibility.

Genesis 2:9 And out of the ground made the LORD God to grow every tree that is pleasant to the sight, and good for food; the tree of life also in the midst of the garden, and the tree of knowledge of good and evil.

Genesis 2:16, 17 And the LORD God commanded the man, saying, Of every tree of the garden thou mayest freely eat: But of the tree of the knowledge of good and evil, thou shalt not eat of it: for in the day that thou eatest thereof thou shalt surely die.

God made man in His own image, this was not a physical image, but this likeness of God is in man's spirit. This image included the right of a free will, the right of choice. This right of choice was given to the angels also, for it was Lucifer's choice to exalt his throne as the throne of God.

Man was given a free will, the right of choice, but he also was given the responsibility to exercise that choice in obedience to God's revealed will. The simple test that God set for that obedience was to forbid Adam and Eve to eat of one tree out of all the trees He had provided, the tree of this knowledge of good and evil.

This brings us to the setting for the most cataclysmic event ever to take place on the face of the earth. Adam and Eve, created in innocence and perfection with no sin in their spirits, no sickness in their bodies, were placed in a beautiful garden paradise with all its lovely creations at their fingertips, and they had dominion. Into this calm scene came Lucifer, now called Satan, the adversary. Homeless, stripped of the splendor and prestige he once knew, Satan was in a rage at God. He wanted revenge. He wanted to strike back. How could he do it? God is invulnerable. He is invincible. There was no way Satan could strike directly at Him.

As Satan saw the sweet communion between God and man, and the love God had for man, Satan formulated his diabolical plan. Having failed to gain dominion in heaven from God, he would take dominion on earth from man. In so doing, he not only would have the worship and adoration he always wanted, he would get back at God by striking at man, the apple of God's eye, His crowning creation.

Satan did not present himself to humankind in the form that has been widely believed for centuries. Nothing could be further from the truth. In the first place, Satan is a spirit, although he can manifest himself in other forms. Secondly, he does not usually advertise his wickedness. Most often he comes in disguise as an angel of light: *"...Satan himself is transformed into an angel of light"* (2 Corinthians 11:14).

To make his entrance into the Garden of Eden for his attack upon God's perfect creation, Satan chose to come in the form of the serpent, not only the most subtle, most cunning of all the creatures, but one of the most beautiful. The serpent at that time was not a snake as we know it today, crawling in the dust; but an upright creation that glittered with beauty. He came in beauty, and he came as an angel of light, to set Adam and Even "straight" about what God had told them:

Genesis 3:1-5 Now the serpent was more subtil than any beast of the field which the LORD God had made. And he said unto the woman, Yea, hath God said, Ye shall not eat of every tree of the garden? And the woman said unto the serpent, We may eat of the fruit of the trees of the garden: But of the fruit of the tree which *is* in the midst of the garden, God hath said, Ye shall not eat of it, neither shall ye touch it, lest ye die. And the serpent said unto the woman, Ye shall not surely die: For God doth know that in the day ye eat thereof, then your eyes shall be opened, and ye shall be as gods, knowing good and evil.

There have been many cartoons and advertisements which depict a lighthearted Eve biting into an apple. The episode of her disobedience to God has been made to look like a "fun" thing. Even more serious-minded individuals and many ministers of God often fail to see the agonizing destruction to humankind inherent in this one seemingly simple act.

Genesis 3:6 And when the woman saw that the tree *was* good for food, and that it *was* pleasant to the eyes, and a tree to be desired to make *one* wise, she took of the fruit thereof, and did eat, and gave also unto her husband with her; and he did eat. Let me stress to you the importance of what transpired here. This was more than a man and a woman eating a piece of fruit out of curiosity or to satisfy their appetites. This is one of the most chilling acts that ever took place. Here was a man, Adam, holding the keys of dominion of this world as given to him by God, and in willful disobedience to God's revealed will, in willful obedience to the influence of Satan, he ate of the fruit which God had forbidden him. In doing so, man handed to Satan, God's archenemy, the keys to the dominion of the world. He bowed to Satan. He gave into Satan's hands what God had put in the hands of man.

With this one act of disobedience, Adam abdicated as the ruler of this world and helped Satan onto the throne of dominion. What Satan had failed to accomplish in heaven with the help of rebellious angels, he accomplished in one fell swoop upon earth with the willful cooperation of man. This is why Satan is described as "god of this world" in Second Corinthians:

2 Corinthians 4:4 In whom the god of this world hath blinded the minds of them which believe not, lest the light of the glorious gospel of Christ, who is the image of God, should shine unto them.

The coup which gave Satan dominion over fallen humankind opened the door in God's perfect creation for imperfection. It not only marked the entrance of sin into this world, but it paved the way for the entrance of two other great evils God never intended for man to have—sickness and death.

This one act of disobedience on man's part and the transfer of the keys of dominion from man to Satan is what set in motion the great spiritual warfare which exists to this very day and is the basis for all the sin, sorrow, and sickness in the world. Every battle man has ever had, or will ever have, is because of this fact. That is why it is so important for us to know how to deal with it as we face the battles of this life and reclaim the dominion God meant for man to have.

Chapter Four
CAN A CHRISTIAN BE DEMON POSSESSED?

This is a big question that many have no idea of the real answer. The answer is no, at least not in the way that we usually think of "possession." Let me explain.

First of all, there is no distinction in the Bible between oppression, possession, vexation, or anything else that demons can do to you. The word used in the New Testament for anyone suffering from demonic pressure was *daimonizomai*. The modern interpretation of this word would be "demonized."

To further understand what it means to be demonized, you might ask: "What kind of spirit is in control of (or ruling) my life any time I react in great fear?" For instance, if you suddenly turn pale, go into a cold sweat, tremble, and start screaming when you become frightened, what kind of spirit would you say is in control of your mind at that moment—

the Spirit of God or the spirit of fear? If you become violently ill when you even think about getting on an airplane, which spirit is ruling your mind at that time? I'll tell you, it sure isn't the Spirit of God.

Then where is God when all of this is happening? You *know* that you've accepted Jesus as your personal Savior. You know that you have received His Holy Spirit. If this is so, then where is He when these vicious fears strike?

Beloved, your Lord has promised that He will never leave you nor forsake you (see Hebrews 13:5). Therefore, He is right there all the time, standing by in your new inner self.

He is waiting for you to call on Him in those moments of hidden terror. He is waiting for you to learn to recognize His Presence within you and to tap into His power so that He might rise up from within you and defeat the enemy.

You see, that perfect seed of Christ's life, which was planted within you when you were born again, can never be possessed, oppressed, or in any way infiltrated by the enemy. It is impregnable, incapable of being assaulted or penetrated by any outside, evil force.

However, that precious seed of Christ's life in your inner man is like a tiny embryo encased by the outer "shell" of your old nature.

During your years of spiritual growth, this outer shell will begin to crack, crumble, and eventually fall away as the "new person" within you starts to grow and emerge. This process is much like a baby chick coming out of its shell. Step by step the chick becomes stronger and stronger as it pecks its way out, until one day it totally breaks through to the outside world.

Through all of this, the chick is being mightily strengthened from within by having to break through its shell. By the time the chick does break through its shell, it is strong enough to cope with its new world. Likewise, you, too, are emerging as a totally new person in Christ. The Word of God assures you:

2 Corinthians 5:17 Therefore if any man *be* in Christ, *he is* a new creature: old things are passed away; behold, all things are become new.

One biblical truth you will come to discover is that no promises in the Bible are simply dumped into our lap. From cover to cover, the Word of God is about pressing through to (and for) God. It is a Book about laboring and overcoming through Christ.

The children of Israel found this out the hard way. From the days of Abraham, God had allotted the Promised Land to them. Yet isn't it strange that they couldn't just walk into it after years in the wilderness, kick up their feet, and say, "Oh, Hallelujah! God gave us this land, and it's ours. We'll just settle down." Why couldn't they do this? Because the Promised Land was filled with enemies, and brother, they had to fight a battle to take every inch of the promise.

It's the same with our soul. Jesus has already paid the price to redeem it, but by the time you were born again, that mind of yours was infested with every kind of fear, negative thought pattern, rotten attitude, and worldly reasoning that the devil could pack into it.

So just as Canaan wasn't automatically purged of the resident enemies when the Israelites walked in, all of your fears didn't get automatically washed from your mind the day you said, "I love You, Jesus." What did happen when you were born again was that you were cleansed from the guilt of all of your sins and fears. You were not automatically freed from the power of sin or the power of fear. That is why there is a spiritual war raging in your life right now:

Ephesians 6:12 For we wrestle not against flesh and blood, but against principalities, against powers, against the rulers of the darkness of this world, against spiritual wickedness in high *places*.

Jesus Christ is coming back for a bride without spot or wrinkle (see Ephesians 5:27). When you came to Him, you were not without spot or wrinkle. Your mind and soul were a mess. This is the reason you must fight to reclaim the territory of your mind by overcoming a foe who has already been defeated.

Yes, Satan was defeated by Jesus. Through the power of Christ in us, we too must conquer him. Through our Lord Jesus Christ, God has given to you all of the authority, the ability, and the power to become perfect in Him. He has given you all that you need to lay hold of Christ's victory and be more than conquerors (see Romans 8:37). You have been fully equipped with everything necessary to grow up into the mature, perfect Bride for His Son.

Obviously, Satan does not want you to use what God has given you. He wants to keep you in bondage to him (through fear), so that you never become an acceptable Bride. The only way Satan can do this is to find a foothold in your unrenewed mind, to "roar" at you with fearful thoughts, and hope you will accept them. The worst thing you can do when this happens is to run back into your shell or give in to these fears.

However, God has no intention of letting you give in or go down to defeat. He intends for you to emerge strong and triumphant. God says:

...And if he draws back and shrinks in fear, My soul has no delight or pleasure in him. Habakkuk 2:3-4.

But our way is not that of those who draw back to eternal misery... but we are of those who believe (who cleave to and trust in and rely on God through Jesus Christ, the Messiah) and by faith preserve the soul (Hebrews 10:38-39 AMP).

I will warn you now that Satan will try to latch onto every fear you have ever had in the past in an effort to press in and strangle that new spiritual life within you. His goal is to see that you never reach spiritual maturity.

Don't be afraid! Think of Satan's demonic spirit of fear as a big, black baboon that is trying to hang onto the "cage" of your old, unrenewed self. There he is, rattling it, shaking it, screeching at you, trying with all of his might to get you to shrink back in fear and stifle that tiny light inside. His aim is to so thoroughly possess your old nature that the new person within you never has a chance. You must resist! This is why spiritual growth is not easy.

The apostle Paul himself said, *"My little children, of whom I travail in birth again until Christ be formed in you"* (Galatians 4:19). As Paul found out, getting people "saved" was the easy part. Getting them to grow up to be spiritually mature and victorious was a different matter. It is not automatic. The apostle John reinforces this when he tells us, *"But as many as received him, to them gave he power to become the sons of God..."* (John 1:12).

Some don't make it. Five (50 percent) of the ten virgins who went out to meet the bridegroom (Jesus) were shut out of the wedding feast (see Matthew 25:1-10). Can you imagine a 50 percent fatality rate in the Church today?

I can.

Why? Because of fear.

So, are you ready to do something about all of those treacherous fears that are haunting your life? If you are, then let's get started.

The first step to overcoming any problem is to understand it. In our case, we must fully understand that the spirit of fear is actually a powerful force for evil which can create or call into being the very thing that is feared. Job experienced this when he said:

Job 3:25 For the thing which I greatly feared is come upon me, and that which I was afraid of is come unto me.

This being so, how does evil power work?

Ever since God created the universe, spiritual powers have had dominion over mental powers, and the powers of the mind have had dominion over the physical realm.

Whatever spirits we choose to accept into our mind will determine what will be manifested in our physical realm. For example, if you choose to allow the spirit of fear in your life, you will think fearful thoughts, speak fearful words, and what you fear will eventually come to pass. If you choose to accept God's spirit of peace, then you will think peaceful thoughts, speak in peace, and create serenity all around you.

Make no mistake. There are only two kinds of spiritual forces in the world—those that are of God (for good) and those that are of Satan (for evil). You have the Spirit above all spirits (the Spirit of God) dwelling deep in your innermost being. The crucial question you must still face daily is, which spirit—the Spirit of God or the spirit of fear—will I choose to accept into my mind today? Which thoughts will I accept or reject?

Be warned that whichever side you permit to control your thoughts, that side will control your entire being.

Romans 6:16 Know ye not, that to whom ye yield yourselves servants to obey, his servants ye are to whom ye obey; whether of sin unto death, or of obedience unto righteousness?

I have often taught that faith is a fact, but faith is also an act. What I have meant is that faith, as a creative spiritual force, is not manifested in the physical realm until you choose with your mind and your will to bring it into being by acting on it.

Fear works the same way. Satan can roar at you all he wants to, but if you refuse to let his fearful thoughts dwell in your mind and refuse to act on them, there's nothing more he can do. He will flee from your resistance!

However, if you choose to act on the suggestions planted by the spirit of fear (or use the words of your mouth to reinforce them), you have released a powerful evil force to start working. What's more, acting and reacting to fear soon becomes a dangerous habit which is very hard to break.

This is why in the Garden of Eden, Satan wasted no time in going after Eve's mind. He knew that if she accepted his suggestions in her mind, these thoughts would then feed her will. Once she chose (with her will) to act on them, she was his.

Chapter Five
COULD A DEMON BE CONTROLLING YOUR LIFE?

There is a large a majority of believers that do not believe that there is demonic power. Demonic power is real. Do you believe it? I know you say that you do, but do you really believe that Satan's demons could be controlling your life right now?

I'm beginning to discover that even very dedicated Christians don't really understand what is happening to them in the spirit world. Think about this, 'There is no total victory in spiritual war until we (as Christians) conquer our enemy who has already been defeated.' Now, I know that Satan is our enemy, and that demons do exist; but if Jesus already defeated them at Calvary two thousand years ago, why do we have to conquer them all over again? How could Satan have any real power over Christians if Jesus has already won?

Unfortunately, this thinking is very common. On one hand, Christians are living lives of torment, walking in bondage and defeat with no real spiritual power. On the other hand, they know God's

Word and have been trained in spiritual warfare, but they have little idea of the power and the seriousness of the war they are in. The bottom line of all their thinking is, Satan has already been stripped of his power. I'm safe because I'm in Jesus' hands.

If this is what you have been telling yourself, then you, too, have been blinded by one of the enemy's most brutal deceptions. Somehow, he has convinced you that all of the problems, illnesses, defeats, depressions, and anxieties in your life have nothing to do with demonic powers. He makes you think that they are all caused by circumstances, your in-laws, the wrong vitamins, a bad childhood, or anything else you can think of!

The fact is that demonic oppression is very real in the Church today.

There is one demon spirit that controls, dominates, possesses, oppresses, vexes, and torments eight out of ten people in the world today, including born-again Christians!

Right now there is an 80 percent chance that this demon spirit is secretly pulling you away from God, destroying your witness for Christ, and choking your growth in the Holy Spirit, and you don't even know it. Can you believe it?

I intend to prove it to you. Let us now turn to the Word of God, for God's infallible Word is the same yesterday, today, and forever.

The Bible says that one day a man came to Jesus and pleaded:
Matthew 17:15 Lord, have mercy on my son: for he is lunatick, and sore vexed: for ofttimes he falleth into the fire, and oft into the water.

What was the boy's problem? Was it psychological? Hereditary? The Bible goes on to plainly state that he was vexed with a demon. For as soon as *"Jesus rebuked the demon in the boy...it left him, and from that moment the boy was well"* (Matthew 17:18 TLB).

Then, in Luke, we learn of a man from Gadara who was more than insane. When he came to meet Jesus, he was homeless, naked, and lived in a cemetery among the tombs. The demons took control of the man so often that even when he was shackled with chains, he simply broke them apart and rushed into the desert completely under the demons' power. When attacks and fits of demonic activity would come upon him, he would throw himself against rocks until his body was cut open and bleeding. When Jesus asked this demon his name, he replied, "Legion," because there were so many! (See Luke 8:27-31.)

Many people in this modern, sophisticated twenty-first century would say, "The poor man probably had a severe hormonal imbalance." Or, "I know that that kind of behavior is the result of a traumatic childhood." Or, "I guess he was just born a 'bad seed'."

That's not what the Bible says. The Bible says it was the work of demon spirits, pure and simple. The Word of God proves that this man was not just a bad seed or someone with a chemical problem, because when he was delivered of all of those foul spirits, he immediately became an outstanding evangelist (see Luke 8:33-39).

We could go on and on, proving in case after case that demonic power was real in Jesus' day. Not only was it real, but it severely tormented, oppressed, possessed, vexed, and controlled many people of biblical times. Demons caused deafness, blindness, and countless other ailments that destroyed the minds and bodies not only of the heathen, but of God's very own people.

The Bible tells us exactly what makes them do these things. It is the same demonic power that tried to murder that mentally deranged boy by throwing him into the fire! Again, we could go on and on with modern-day examples of demonic power and not even uncover the tip of the iceberg.

In Jesus' day, the reality of demonic power was never questioned. People knew it existed, pure and simple. The only thing that amazed them was that there was finally someone around who had the power over the devil to do something about it. And do something He did. Jesus dealt with all of these gruesome situations in short order. How? With power and authority He commanded each one of those foul spirits to leave, and they did!

The public was astounded:

Mark 1:27 And they were all amazed, insomuch that they questioned among themselves, saying, What thing is this? what new doctrine *is* this? for with authority commandeth he even the unclean spirits, and they do obey him.

By now you may be saying,

Let me ask you a question. Do we have people in the Church today who are deaf? People who can't speak? People who have mental problems? People who are constantly ill?

Jesus has plainly shown us that many of these afflictions are a direct result of demonic oppression. (See Matthew 12:28,43; Mark 1:23,26; 7:25; 9:17-26; Luke 4:33; 8:29; 9:42 and 13:11.) In addition, we see the utter devastation caused by broken homes, child abuse, and divorce, which are rampant in the Church today. These are the very things that God sent His Son to this earth to destroy.

...For this purpose the Son of God was manifested, that He might destroy the works of the devil (1 John 3:8 NKJV).

He then put all of the keys to spiritual power in our hands to finish the job. He has given us power over all of the power of the enemy (see Luke 10:19). Then why haven't we done something about all of those tormented, demon-oppressed brothers and sisters, sitting right next to us in the pews, as we listen to sermons about love week after week? My Bible says that just as Jesus is in heaven (the Everlasting Conqueror), so are we to be right now in this world (1 John 4:17).

Who is Jesus? He is the Victor. He is a Man of war against all of the destructive forces of the devil.

What are we? We are so bound and oppressed that I am concerned that many Christians are literally on their way to being spit out of His mouth! (See Revelation 3:16.)

Today the Lord is urgently sounding the alarm, trying to make us see that many people in the Church who have assumed that they will be part of the Marriage Supper of the Lamb could instead be cast out of His Kingdom if they insist on living with the oppressive forces that are binding them and destroying Christ's Church. These oppressive forces are making you, as a Christian, both helpless and useless.

I want to read to you one of the most chilling stories in the Word of God. It is a story that haunts me day and night—a story that keeps me awake, grieving for God's blinded, oppressed, dominated, and controlled people.

I know of nothing that shows how a Christian can be rendered helpless, uselessly bound by Satan, more than the story Jesus Himself tells in Matthew 25:14-30. Open your Bible with me now as the Lord reveals to us the horrifying truth of how Satan oppresses God's people in the Church.

I do not know of another power that can render you as helpless and useless, that can tie your hands, bind your mind, control, vex, and torment your soul like the spirit of fear!

The apostle Paul warned Timothy, *"For God hath not given us the spirit of fear; but of power, and of love, and of a sound mind"* (2 Timothy 1:7). The Word also tells us that, *"fear hath torment"* (1 John 4:18). Since fear is a tormenting spirit, we know that it does not come from God. And if it does not come from God, there is only one other source fear can come from, and that is from Satan!

It is the devil's goal to keep you oppressed by fear, to prevent you from doing the will of God, and to keep you from being used by God in the gifts of the Spirit. Fear is one way that Satan keeps us in bondage to self. When God gives you a gift of His Spirit to give to others, Satan uses fear to make you think: This might not be God. It's probably just me, and I'll make a fool of myself. I'd better hold back.

Fear is also the devil's tool to keep us in bondage to the opinions of man. We are afraid of what people will think or say about us. We become afraid that we might not be accepted in our denomination if we go all the way for God.

I know of nothing that binds, vexes, torments, and keeps us from doing God's will more than fear. When we attend a spiritual meeting, God moves upon our heart to give money to reach the lost. As soon as we get home, Satan attacks: You can't give that amount. It's too much. You were just being emotional. What will happen if you get cancer or lose your job? You have so little money in the bank. Fear strikes, and God is robbed. Satan has won the victory. The door is now open for the enemy to come in and hinder the glorious promises of God. The unholy spirit of fear takes control. The Kingdom suffers.

Remember that judgment begins in the house of God (see 1 Peter 4:17). If you go down to defeat because of giving in to the spirit of fear, what will you say when you stand before God?

Friend, if you have ever made a pledge to God and not fulfilled that vow, I urge you to do so before you go one step further. I don't want you to stand before the Master and hear what the unprofitable servant heard. Jesus told him, *"Depart from me,"* and he was cast into outer darkness (see Luke 13:27).

We are to be ruled by love for our Lord, never by fear! The Book of Ecclesiastes tells us:

Let us each determine today to overcome all fear so that we might glorify God by triumphantly saying to Him, *"Praise waiteth for thee, O God, in Sion: and unto thee shall the vow be performed"* (Psalm 65:1).

Beloved, it's harvest time! This is not a fire drill! It's the real thing! Jesus is coming! Let us all get our house in order quickly and, using all of the resources at our disposal, move on to total victory in Him.

This unprofitable servant was afraid to use the resources that God had given him to use. He refused to use the tools that God had given him to overcome his fear. However, as sad as this story sounds, it is nothing compared to what is going on with God's servants today. If you don't believe me, there are Christians whose lives are fruitless and in complete bondage to the spirit of fear.

Revelations 21:8 But the fearful, and unbelieving, and the abominable, and murderers, and whoremongers, and sorcerers, and idolaters, and all liars, shall have their part in the lake which burneth with fire and brimstone: which is the second death.

I know this is not a passage that many of you have underlined in your Bible. Yet it is just as true as all of the promises for prosperity, health, and happiness that we're so fond of. Believe me, if God's Word says something, we have two choices: We can either take it very seriously, or we can fall into deceit. Which do you choose?

When you stand before your Lord on that final day, are you going to face Him with the many "treasures" of lost souls that you've won and nurtured, or with a lot of feeble excuses of why you were afraid to step out?

Luke 12:48 But he that knew not, and did commit things worthy of stripes, shall be beaten with few *stripes*. For unto whomsoever much is given, of him shall be much required: and to whom men have committed much, of him they will ask the more.

Are you going to say, "Yes, Lord. I obeyed Your every command. I took every tool You gave me, overcame my fears, and was victorious for You." Or are you going to say, "Well, I know Your Word said, 'Fear not,' but I didn't think that applied to me. You see, I had a burden to pray for the sick, but I was afraid to learn to drive, so I never got far from my house." Or, "I was the shy type, so I never got into witnessing. I did play the piano in Sunday school, though. Wasn't that enough?" Or, "I was afraid that if I tithed, I wouldn't have enough for myself. I was afraid to trust You to provide for me."

So what was the unprofitable servant's excuse for being afraid? Fear of poverty! He told the Lord:

Matthew 25:25 And I was afraid, and went and hid thy talent in the earth: lo, *there* thou hast *that is* thine.

What about you? Are you in bondage to the fear of giving because you're afraid that the Lord might ask you for more, or that the well will run dry?

Many of you are in such bondage to fear that you are afraid to receive healing from God. I tell you, the Church today is being ruled by a spirit of fear. Because of this, hundreds of thousands of "born-again" Christians, who think they're in good shape with the Lord, are sinking fast into "unprofitable servanthood." This includes pastors, ministers, and evangelists. Yes, the spirit of fear is not only ruling the pews, it's in the pulpit too.

Chapter Six

GOD'S ARMOR AGAINST SATAN'S ATTACK

You may have heard several sermons on the full armor of God. Well until we are fully protected from the enemy we need to full comprehend God's armor. Because of the peculiar nature of our enemy, the devil, God has provided peculiar armor for our protection and peculiar weapons with which to battle him.

We have pointed out that there are only two sides in this warfare that deal with all of life, and we have emphasized that this is a spiritual battle. We also have emphasized that the outcome is never in doubt. God has all power and all things are under His control, and we are victors because of Him. Satan has no power over us at all.

This is contingent, however, on one thing: We must fight by God's rules. He has not left us in doubt of these rules. He has made every provision for our welfare in battle, our growth even in the midst of the warfare, and for our ultimate and complete triumph over all the forces of the devil.

What most people are prone to forget is the purely spiritual nature of the proceedings. Sometimes we allow ourselves to be drawn into conflicts with people, or with things, or even with ourselves. Second Timothy 2:25 speaks of *"those that oppose themselves."* When we forget who the real enemy is, we misdirect our firepower and it is dissipated without really getting to the root of the problem at hand.

God has carefully outlined a complete set of armor for our protection and use in the battle and has set these forth in Ephesians 6:

Ephesians 6:11-18 *Put on the whole armour of God, that ye may be able to stand against the wiles of the devil. For we wrestle not against flesh and blood, but against principalities, against powers, against the rulers of the darkness of this world, against spiritual wickedness in high places.* Wherefore take unto you the whole armour of God, that ye may be able to withstand in the evil day, and having done all, to stand. Stand therefore, having your loins girt about with truth, and having on the breastplate of righteousness; And your feet shod with the preparation of the gospel of peace; Above all, taking the shield of faith, wherewith ye shall be able to quench all the fiery darts of the wicked. And take the helmet of salvation, and the sword of the Spirit, which is the word of God: Praying always with all prayer and supplication in the Spirit, and watching thereunto with all perseverance and supplication for all saints;

The reason we must put on the whole or entire armor of God is very simple: In ourselves we are no match for the devil at all. Not the slightest. It is only in the strength of God that we can even stand. We must take our place in His complete protection and not leave one spot uncovered for Satan's touch. *"Neither give place to the devil"* (Ephesians 4:27)

Completely armored by God, however, we will stand in complete invulnerability to Satan's attack. *"...When it is all over, you will still be standing up"* (Ephesians 6:13 TLB). We must use every bit of the armor that God has given us so that not one spot is vulnerable to the attack of the enemy in any form.

Here is the armor God has provided us:
1. Having your loins girt about with truth
2. The breastplate of righteousness
3. Your feet shod with the preparation of the Gospel of Peace
4. The shield of faith

5. The helmet of salvation

6. The sword of the Spirit, which is the Word of God

Let us examine this armor one piece at a time.

YOUR LOINS GIRT ABOUT WITH TRUTH

Truth is our undergirding. Though antagonists in many worldly battles and disagreements fight with lies, bluffing, exaggeration, and evasion, our undergirding is ever the truth of God's Word. Not only is His Word true, but He is Truth. Jesus said: *"I am the way, the truth, and the life..."* (John 14:6).

Since Jesus and Satan are opposites, it is safe and true to say that as Christ is the way, Satan is the wrong way. As Jesus is the truth, Satan is a liar and the father of lies. As Jesus is the life, Satan is the bearer of spiritual death.

John 8:44 Ye are of *your* father the devil, and the lusts of your father ye will do. He was a murderer from the beginning, and abode not in the truth, because there is no truth in him. When he speaketh a lie, he speaketh of his own: for he is a liar, and the father of it.

If we make use of lies, we are using Satan's own tools, and certainly we are no match for him in that respect. Jesus is truth. We need never be afraid of truth, and we need never be afraid of truth failing us in any way. We can stand on any promise of God with unwavering faith that what He has promised, that will He do.

2 Corinthians 1:20 For all the promises of God in him *are* yea, and in him Amen, unto the glory of God by us.

1 Kings 8:56 Blessed *be* the LORD, that hath given rest unto his people Israel, according to all that he promised: there hath not failed one word of all his good promise, which he promised by the hand of Moses his servant.

In order to be girt with the truth, we must know the truth. We not only must know Jesus as the personification of Truth, but the whole Word of God as truth. There is no way to stand on what God has said if we do not know what He has said. Therefore, a personal knowledge of the Truth, Jesus Christ, and a knowledge of God's written truth are essentials in the battle at hand.

Satan is a wonder-worker and is capable of performing lying wonders designed to turn souls away from the truth. Those who do not love and hold to the truth are open to the snares of Satan and are destined for failure.

2 Thessalonians 2:9-12 *Even him,* whose coming is after the working of Satan with all power and signs and lying wonders, And

with all deceivableness of unrighteousness in them that perish; because they received not the love of the truth, that they might be saved. And for this cause God shall send them strong delusion, that they should believe a lie: That they all might be damned who believed not the truth, but had pleasure in unrighteousness.

King Ahab fell into the snare of satanic delusion because he continually had shunned the truth of God. Those who do not love the truth, or do not want the truth, are defeated before the battle is begun. Truth is our only sure footing.

THE BREASTPLATE OF RIGHTEOUSNESS

Righteousness goes hand in hand with truth, as in the passage from Second Thessalonians quoted above. Righteousness, as a breastplate, speaks of guarding the heart against all unrighteousness. Right standing before God is essential to the flow of His power in our lives.

There have been many cases where people of impure motives have sought to use the power of God without being qualified to use it. Those who attempt such folly not only will fail to obtain the desired results, but will run into serious difficulties because of their efforts to do so.

In Acts 19, we read of the seven sons of Sceva:

Acts 19:13-16 Then certain of the vagabond Jews, exorcists, took upon them to call over them which had evil spirits the name of the Lord Jesus, saying, We adjure you by Jesus whom Paul preacheth. And there were seven sons of *one* Sceva, a Jew, *and* chief of the priests, which did so. And the evil spirit answered and said, Jesus I know, and Paul I know; but who are ye? And the man in whom the evil spirit was leaped on them, and overcame them, and prevailed against them, so that they fled out of that house naked and wounded.

These men went through the same actions they had seen Paul go through, and used the same type of words which Paul had spoken. They even used the Name of Jesus. However, Satan knows when we are not shielded with the spiritual breastplate which guards our hearts. The battle went against the sons of Sceva, and they were forced to flee in wounded dishonor.

Another instance occurred when Simon, who had been a sorcerer, saw the power of the Holy Spirit in the lives of the apostles, and sought to purchase that power for himself:

Acts 8:18, 19 And when Simon saw that through laying on of the apostles' hands the Holy Ghost was given, he offered them money, Saying, Give me also this power, that on whomsoever I lay hands, he may receive the Holy Ghost.

Peter's scathing denunciation was:

Acts 8:20-23 But Peter said unto him, Thy money perish with thee, because thou hast thought that the gift of God may be purchased with money. Thou hast neither part nor lot in this matter: for thy heart is not right in the sight of God. For I perceive that thou art in the gall of bitterness, and *in* the bond of iniquity.

We realize that our own righteousness is of no avail. Yet we must enter into the righteousness that is in Christ Jesus if we are to utilize His power.

Isaiah 64:6 But we are all as an unclean *thing,* and all our righteousnesses *are* as filthy rags; and we all do fade as a leaf; and our iniquities, like the wind, have taken us away.

John 15:7 If ye abide in me, and my words abide in you, ye shall ask what ye will, and it shall be done unto you.

It is impossible to walk in the Spirit of God if we are under condemnation.

Romans 8:1 *There is* therefore now no condemnation to them which are in Christ Jesus, who walk not after the flesh, but after the Spirit.

While being careful that Satan not cause us to unjustly condemn ourselves, or that we fail to forgive ourselves for past wrongs for which God has forgiven us, we must also be careful that we walk in such a way that we do not bring real condemnation upon ourselves. When we do fail God, we must seek restored communion with Him and righteousness in Him at once.

John 1:9 *That* was the true Light, which lighteth every man that cometh into the world.

THE PREPARATION OF THE GOSPEL OF PEACE

This preparation is exactly what you are doing as you study this text. That this admonition is connected with the feet shows willingness, even eagerness, to go. Jesus' last command to His disciples before His ascension was: *"...Go ye into all the world, and preach the gospel to every creature"* (Mark 16:15). The preparation of the gospel of peace even makes our feet beautiful:

Isaiah 52:7 How beautiful upon the mountains are the feet of him that bringeth good tidings, that publisheth peace; that bringeth good tidings of good, that publisheth salvation; that saith unto Zion, Thy God reigneth!

Having the power of God will profit no one—neither yourself, God, nor the person in need if you do not obey Christ's command to "go." Because many people have misinterpreted the "go," they have misdirected their efforts, not realizing that all can fulfill this command. Many are not called to go to foreign fields, or even to leave their hometowns, but every child of God is called to go into all the world of their own influence to spread the Gospel of Peace with which we have been prepared and shod.

Whatever your sphere of influence—whether you are a housewife, a professional person, or a laborer—be ready and prepared to go share the power of God in your life with others who need your ministry.

THE SHIELD OF FAITH

Paul said that "above all" this is to be part of our armor. *"But without faith it is impossible to please him..."* (Hebrews 11:6). Without faith, we have no hold on the truth. Without faith, we cannot appropriate the righteousness that is in Jesus Christ. Without faith, we cannot shod ourselves with the preparation of the Gospel of Peace.

It is easy to see how important faith is when we consider again the case of Job. Under fiery attack by Satan (though unknown to him), Job lost everything that he had except his faith. *"Though he slay me, yet will I trust him..."* (Job 13:15). Job's faith held out until every one of Satan's fiery darts had hit against it and fallen away. Job not only remained unharmed, but was left in far better circumstances than he had been before those darts were fired at him. Faith not only quenches the fiery darts of the enemy sent against us, but equips us to send our fiery weaponry against him, since by faith in Christ we are enabled to do exploits for Him.

Peter was just one of the apostles who had a ministry of miracles, yet Peter attributed all his power where it rightfully belonged:

Acts 3:12 And when Peter saw *it,* he answered unto the people, Ye men of Israel, why marvel ye at this? or why look ye so earnestly on us, as though by our own power or holiness we had made this man to walk?

Acts 3:16 And his name through faith in his name hath made this man strong, whom ye see and know: yea, the faith which is by him hath given him this perfect soundness in the presence of you all.

THE HELMET OF SALVATION

A helmet offers protection for the head. Our armor is not only righteousness, which is of the heart, but a mind that knows the salvation of God and is submitted to Him. The mind that is not stayed upon God becomes a playground for Satan's suggestions to pull us away from the truth into areas of wrong decisions and actions. Our minds continually must be under the blood of Jesus, which saved us from sin in the first place.

2 Timothy 1:7 For God hath not given us the spirit of fear; but of power, and of love, and of a sound mind.

A person who dwells on negatives will never amount to a positive power force for God. God Himself has told us what kind of thoughts we must hold:

Philippians 4:8 Finally, brethren, whatsoever things are true, whatsoever things *are* honest, whatsoever things *are* just, whatsoever things *are* pure, whatsoever things *are* lovely, whatsoever things *are* of good report; if *there be* any virtue, and if *there be* any praise, think on these things.

THE SWORD OF THE SPIRIT

Truth not only is our standing place, it is our defense to cut down the attacks of the enemy when he comes against us. It is also our offensive weapon to cut into Satan's very territory. We are completely safe and sheltered in God for:

Isaiah 54:17 No weapon that is formed against thee shall prosper; and every tongue *that* shall rise against thee in judgment thou shalt condemn. This *is* the heritage of the servants of the LORD, and their righteousness *is* of me, saith the LORD.

    Clothed in the full armor of God, prepared to stand despite the battle, we move on in our warfare from defensive to offensive to learn how to invade Satan's territory and come away with unspeakable spoils of triumphant battle!

Chapter Seven
LOCATING THE ENEMY

We are facing one of the worst times where we must know where the enemy lies in things. All truth is parallel. That means that whatever is happening over here in the natural world is also happening in a similar manner in the spiritual world. The first rule of warfare, whether it is earthly or spiritual, is that you must locate your enemy.

One of the main reasons that the Church has failed to press in and take this world for Jesus Christ is because it has made converts, not disciples. It has begotten sons...but it has not made them soldiers who know how to wage effective warfare. God has called for a trained and motivated army, and we have failed to mobilize for the battle He has called us to.

The purpose of this is that we may be trained, equipped, and mobilized to wage effective warfare with our adversary (satan) for dominion over this world. It is designed to enable God's people to turn the stance of Christianity from a defensive holding position to an all-out offensive to conquer in God's Name.

One of the very first rules of successful warfare is that we must know our enemy. We must locate him and concentrate our firepower upon him; otherwise our efforts will be dissipated and ineffective.

The world today is in a state of fear. They know there are powerful enemies at work, but they do not know who or what these enemies are, where to look for them, or how to overcome them. Many of our politicians, sociologists, and psychologists have a very pessimistic outlook on the future. One prominent scientist said, "We give the world ten years." Many leaders agree that "things" cannot go on in the same vein in which they are now progressing.

Our nation is afraid. The world is afraid. People possess a fearful "looking after" concerning the things that are to come upon the face of the earth such as Jesus prophesied in Luke 21.

Luke 21:26 Men's hearts failing them for fear, and for looking after those things which are coming on the earth: for the powers of heaven shall be shaken.

People are afraid all of our water systems will be so polluted that we will not have fresh, clear water to drink anymore. There are already many shortages of food throughout the world and predictions of famine are ominous. The bleakest part of the picture on top of all this is that sin is completely rampant. Evil is with us on an unprecedented scale—rising crime rates, increased violence, murders, mayhem, robbery, sex crimes, drug addiction—all are on the upswing.

God told me: "There are spirits loosed that have been assigned the devilish task of tearing down the structure and the society of this nation, and the sooner you realize you are not dealing with men or with political ideologies, the sooner you will have the victory." There are spirits that are loose in the world.

Let me ask you a question: How can you fight an enemy you have not located? How can you fight an enemy when you close your eyes and pretend that he does not exist?

There are spirits loose in the world, spirits who have been given the diabolical assignment of tearing down the structure, the foundation of this nation and the nations of the world—the Constitution, the Bible, prayer, and everything that is holy. If every minister, Leader, mother, and father had known the truth about spirits being visited upon our world, they would have saved themselves the chaos and the agony they went through with their children.

One of the cardinal rules of success in any field is that you must deal with people and things as they are, not as you wish them to be. In the face of all the problems and perplexities that come upon us, we must never fail to realize that we are not really dealing with men. We are not dealing with political ideologies. We are not dealing with things! I have no ax to grind with communism, because to me, communism is a defeated enemy. That is not the real problem, or the real issue.

Our warfare is not with men. It is not with the social systems of our day. It is not with political ideologies. We are not in a natural battle; we are in a spiritual conflict. The scripture tells us:

Ephesians 6:12 For we wrestle not against flesh and blood, but against principalities, against powers, against the rulers of the darkness of this world, against spiritual wickedness in high *places.*

In addition to fear, there is also great confusion over our nation. Hardly any political leader will stand up and agree with another on any subject, whether it is economics, sociological problems, foreign policy or any other field. There is great perplexity among our leaders.

Confusion is a spirit. There is a spirit of confusion in the religious world as well as in the political. It exists in denominations, as well as in the lives of individual believers. It is a spirit.

Fear is a spirit. There is a spirit of fear pervading the very atmosphere on an unprecedented scale. People are afraid of so many things. Some of the ills they fear are imaginary, but many are very, very real. People's hearts actually are failing them from fear of circumstances.

Frustration is a spirit. There is total frustration on every hand. I was told by a leading person in the financial world that many presidents of banks in this country are afraid of what is going to come economically. They are trying to sell their holdings to European and foreign interests. I do not say that to scare you, but so that you will know the total, hopeless frustration that exists at the highest levels of our so-called intelligentsia.

Promiscuousness is a spirit. Promiscuousness exists in the very air. The lowering of moral and spiritual standards has reached the point where it no longer is considered immoral to sell the worst kind of literature openly on the streets of this nation and most other nations of the world.

Two boys can walk into a courtroom in this country and demand a marriage license to be married as husband and husband. The "gay liberation" of homosexuality receives mass television and press exposure to propagate this code of conduct on our nation. Many people are now convinced that we must uphold, protect, and even standardize the "rights" of homosexuals.

There are an estimated 4 million homosexuals in North America. It is estimated that fifteen percent of the total population of San Francisco, one of our largest cities, is homosexual. In that city, the public school curriculum includes a course which presents homosexuality as an "alternative lifestyle." It is a spirit of promiscuousness.

These are just a few of the evil spirits loose in the so-called civilized countries of North America which God revealed to me.

God made known to me that when we realize, as servants of God and as the Church of Jesus Christ, that we are not dealing with men or ideologies, but with the unseen spirit world, we will have the greatest victory this world has ever seen in the Name of Jesus.

We are not in a natural conflict; we are in a spiritual conflict. It cannot be solved by Washington, D.C; It cannot be resolved by religious or political gimmicks, or by any natural means that man can contrive. It can only be men and women who have power with God, and by men and women who can prevail over the unseen forces of this world.

When you really absorb this revelation, you will have solid understanding beneath your feet for the power to march forward, knowing in whom you have believed. Your life will never be the same again. You will know how to deal with the spirits of rebellion, confusion, frustration, turmoil, lust, promiscuousness, sin, dope, unconcern, selfishness, criticism, fear, anxiety, and many thousands of other spirits which have been loosed upon our world.

Because of this, many modern-day Christians are so confused that they no longer know the will of God. They do not know where to go, what to do, or where to turn. They do not know what decisions to make or in which direction to go.

Many denominations—even strong evangelicals—choose to take the easy road out. They choose either to ignore these conditions or to place them in the hands of the psychologists. They explain that the unusual power of the Holy Spirit present in the lives of the early Church ceased, and therefore we no longer are required to deal from a standpoint of a supernatural demonstration of God's power.

The apostle Paul knew nothing of that frustration and confusion when he confessed:

1 Corinthians 2:4, 5 And my speech and my preaching *was* not with enticing words of man's wisdom, but in demonstration of the Spirit and of power: That your faith should not stand in the wisdom of men, but in the power of God.

He also declared:

2 Timothy 1:12 For the which cause I also suffer these things: nevertheless I am not ashamed: for I know whom I have believed, and am persuaded that he is able to keep that which I have committed unto him against that day.

There was no confusion in his mind when he wrote:

Romans 8:35 Who shall separate us from the love of Christ? *shall* tribulation, or distress, or persecution, or famine, or nakedness, or peril, or sword?

Romans 8:37 Nay, in all these things we are more than conquerors through him that loved us.

All truth is parallel. As evil is a spirit, good is also a spirit. As hate is a spirit which has infiltrated and ruled the nations of this world, so love is a spirit.

As frustration and confusion are spirits, so is steadfastness. Sickness is a spirit. It is a result of the curse. God never intended for man's eyes to become dim, his ears to become weak, or even for him to lose his hair. God intended for man to live forever. He never intended for man to die. Man was created in the image of God.

There are three things God never intended for man to possess:
1. Sin
2. Sickness
3. Death

The Bible says we are created in the image of God. Through disobedience, the spirit of sin came into the world, and as a result of sin, the spirits of sickness and death.

Salvation is also a spirit.

There are many pastors who will testify that they have preached a message that had nothing to do with salvation, but suddenly they would give an altar call and people would receive Christ as Savior. For three, four, or five weeks in a row, people would be saved in the congregation. There seemed to be a spirit of salvation loosed upon the congregation!

There have been times in a church when there would be two or three services in a row with a special anointing for divine healing. The preacher did not bring it. He did not create it or even especially teach on it. It just seemed to come. That is because healing is a spirit.

When Jesus asked the Samaritan woman for a drink of water as related in John 4, the woman asked Him a question: "Tell me this, if You are a prophet," she said, "You say that we ought to worship God at the Temple in the city of Jerusalem. We Samaritans say that we should worship God in this mountain. Where do You say I am supposed to worship?"

Jesus had the answer. He declared:

John 4:23, 24 But the hour cometh, and now is, when the true worshippers shall worship the Father in spirit and in truth: for the Father seeketh such to worship him. God *is* a Spirit: and they that worship him must worship *him* in spirit and in truth.

God is not confined to a stained-glass window, a robed choir, the stone architecture of a cathedral, or to any historic spot. He is not bound to our traditions, forms, or formalities of worship.

God is not limited to time or space. That is why we can pray in North America and God can answer prayer in India or Africa. There is no limit of time or space because God is a Spirit. He is everywhere present at the same time!

Man is also a spirit. Man is created in the image of God: *"God said, Let us make man in our image, after our likeness..."* (Genesis 1:26). This image of God, however, is not in the physical features of man. It is in the spirit. God gave him (man) a free moral will with the ability to rule his spirit.

The image of God is within us. Because man was created in God's spiritual image, God put him here with divine authority to rule the earth. In this respect, people are like angels. God created the angels with the right of choice. Satan, who formerly was one of the highest-ranking angels, exercised this choice to rebel against God. One third of the angels exercised their choice to follow Satan and were cast out of heaven with him.

Tragically, man used this spiritual image, this right of choice, to make a wrong choice, to disobey God! God had told Adam:

Genesis 2:17 But of the tree of the knowledge of good and evil, thou shalt not eat of it: for in the day that thou eatest thereof thou shalt surely die.

When Adam disobeyed God and sinned, he opened the door for humankind to reap three things that God did not intend for man to possess—sin, sickness, and death. Adam did not die physically on that very day, but he died spiritually. First Corinthians 15:22 says that, "...*in Adam all die.*" It also says that, "...*in Christ shall all be made alive.*" As with Adam, humankind experienced spiritual death, but Christ offers the opportunity to be reborn spiritually.

It is the spiritual part of man that is in God's image. Man is not his physical body. The body returns to dust from whence it came. It is the spirit, God's image, that is the real you, that will live on through eternity. To know this truth is to have located our enemy, to have pinpointed the crux of every conflict. We are not in a natural battle in our problems, in our sicknesses, anxieties, fears, and frustrations. We are in a spiritual warfare in the spirit world. This is the root cause of every problem, every battle, every fear, every frustration we have.

If you walk by a pond and see a fowl with a beak swimming on it, and the sound that a fowl makes is "quack, quack, quack," common sense tells you that fowl is a duck. You call it a duck because it looks like a duck, swims like a duck, acts like a duck, and sounds like a duck.

When things come upon humankind today that look and act like demon power and fulfill the scriptural description, we do not need to be afraid to call them exactly what they are!

Many people are afraid to identify the world of demon power, because they do not have any idea how to deal with it. They do not know how to go in, press the battle against the enemy, and defeat him in the spirit world! If we can use our psychology and sociology to call insanity, criminality, and perversity an "emotional distress resulting from a maladjusted childhood," or if we can use some other theory to justify the problems which plague our generation, then it can be dealt with in the natural mind. This approach, however, will never find a permanent cure, because the problem is a spiritual problem.

If we define the problem as it really is—the spiritual power of Satan which has gotten into lives through the original entrance of sin—we can deal with it as a sinister spiritual power at the root cause. We can go in with the supernatural power of God, the anointing of the Holy Spirit, and defeat the enemy in the Name of Jesus.

The Church today is at a critical junction in history. The road the Church follows is running into an attack by the devil as never before. The road that crosses ours is the devil's power. Because Satan knows that he has but a short season, the Church is facing a challenge of the devil's power it has never faced before.

However, I know beyond a shadow of a doubt how to meet that challenge. God said: *"...upon this rock* (Jesus) *I will build my church; and the gates of hell shall not prevail against it"* (Matthew 16:18).

We are not just in a holding war, the "hold the fort" kind that some churches sing about, hanging on by the skin of our teeth. Ours is an aggressive war, an offensive strategy. We must take the initiative to invade Satan's own territory, carry the battle to his field, overcome him on every hand, and come out of the battle with the spoils of victory held aloft in the hands of a triumphant Church—in the Name and power of Jesus Christ.

There is something that you possess in your life as a Christian of which the devil is deathly afraid. He is no match for it. It is your ultimate assurance of total victory. As God opens to you the revelation of the New Anointing, you are going to have prayer victories such as you have never before experienced. You will experience victories in your life and see them in the lives of your loved ones as never before.

We know who the enemy is, and God has given us the tools of victory. By His power we will take the battleground for God. Total victory is yours!

Chapter Eight
SATAN'S FIELD OF ACTIVITY

Where is satan's field of activity? If God did not cast Satan down to have dominion over this earth, where did He cast him and where is his seat of authority? The book of Job gives a remarkable picture of the wide sphere of activity which Satan enjoys.

Job 1:6, 7 Now there was a day when the sons of God came to present themselves before the LORD, and Satan came also among them. And the LORD said unto Satan, Whence comest thou? Then Satan answered the LORD, and said, From going to and fro in the earth, and from walking up and down in it.

It is immediately apparent that Satan has access both to God's Presence and to the whole range of the earth. Though his activities differ in those two places, his aim is always the same—attack!

What he does before God's Presence is to accuse God, to accuse God's Word, and to accuse God's people. *"...which accused them before our God day and night"* (Revelation 12:10). That is what he was doing to Job at the instance quoted above.

Now, what is Satan doing on earth? He is creating the situations that enable him to accuse God by tempting, harassing, tormenting, and attacking man in any way he can. Peter tells us that Satan's travels up and down this world are those of a roaring lion.

1 Peter 5:8 Be sober, be vigilant; because your adversary the devil, as a roaring lion, walketh about, seeking whom he may devour: Paul tells us he exercises great cunning: *"...Satan himself is transformed into an angel of light"* (2 Corinthians 11:14). The motivation is still the same.

From this picture we get of Satan's widespread evil activities, it would be easy to draw the conclusion that, like God, Satan is omnipresent. This is not so. To know and understand that fact will help us to understand how much greater God is than Satan and how much greater our power against him.

1 John 4:4 Ye are of God, little children, and have overcome them: because greater is he that is in you, than he that is in the world.

We have already seen that Satan is not eternal, and now we see that he is not present everywhere at once. How can we then explain the wide scope of evil which is experienced in all the world at the same time? It is because Satan has a large following of fallen angels or demon spirits to help him carry out his activities.

Ephesians 6:12 For we wrestle not against flesh and blood, but against principalities, against powers, against the rulers of the darkness of this world, against spiritual wickedness in high *places*.

This scripture clearly shows a multiplicity of evil beings—principalities, powers, and rulers. A principality is the state and authority of a prince. Therefore it is apparent that Satan has set up governments and divisions of territory among various rulers. If there are rulers, there must also be those who are ruled, and so it is difficult to even estimate how many evil beings Satan has in his service.

A faint insight is given in the story of the madman of Gadara whom Jesus delivered from demon possession (see Mark 5:1-15; Luke

8:26-35). When Jesus asked the madman his name, he said it was *Legion*, because many devils had entered into him (see Luke 8:30).

"Legion" is a military term. At the time of the Scripture, the term was used by the Roman military to designate a military unit of 3,000 to 6,000 trained and armed men. Use of the term here would indicate not only a large number of demons, but that they were in military ranks of varying authority. We do not know exactly how many demons possessed the man of Gadara, but certainly enough to possess an entire herd of 2,000 swine and cause them to violently destroy themselves (see Mark 5:13).

Despite the number and strength of Satan's legions, however, we need not fear the outcome of the battle.

Revelations 12:4 And his tail drew the third part of the stars of heaven, and did cast them to the earth: and the dragon stood before the woman which was ready to be delivered, for to devour her child as soon as it was born.

From Revelation 12:4 and ensuing verses, we get the figure that Satan took a third of heaven's angels with him when he rebelled. That means two-thirds remained faithful to God—twice as many as Satan has. There are other great pluses to these figures: God is omnipresent and since He is Creator, He could easily create all the angels needed for any service. Even without angels, God Himself is Almighty, and just His Word is able to meet every need.

Though this study is not the study of good angels, let us mention briefly their use by God. Angels ministered to Jesus after He underwent His temptation at the hands of Satan, *"Then the devil leaveth Him, and, behold, angels came and ministered unto Him"* (Matthew 4:11). Satan knew God's promise to Jesus was that angels would protect Him.

Matthew 4:6 And saith unto him, If thou be the Son of God, cast thyself down: for it is written, He shall give his angels charge concerning thee: and in *their* hands they shall bear thee up, lest at any time thou dash thy foot against a stone.

Likewise, the angels of God minister to us and protect us:
Psalms 34:7 The angel of the LORD encampeth round about them that fear him, and delivereth them.

Hebrews 1:7 And of the angels he saith, Who maketh his angels spirits, and his ministers a flame of fire.

God administers His angels from heaven where His throne is above all.

Satan's hordes are described as the *"rulers of the darkness of this world"* (Ephesians 6:12). This term, as well as the description in the book of Revelation, reveals that his headquarters are in the depths of the earth.

Revelation 9:1 tells of the star that fell from heaven to earth and was given the key of the bottomless pit. From this pit, he will let forth unspeakable creatures during the tribulation period to torment men.

Revelations 9:11 And they had a king over them, *which is* the angel of the bottomless pit, whose name in the Hebrew tongue *is* Abaddon, but in the Greek tongue hath *his* name Apollyon.

Also, Revelation 11:7 tells us that the beast as the Antichrist will come out of the bottomless pit.

Revelations 11:7 And when they shall have finished their testimony, the beast that ascendeth out of the bottomless pit shall make war against them, and shall overcome them, and kill them.

It seems certain, therefore, that in the darkness of the earth's depths is where the throne room of Satan is located. Some have held that his throne is in the "heavenlies"—not God's place of abode, heaven, but earth's atmosphere. They use as their authority for this the scripture that speaks of "spiritual wickedness in high places."

Without a doubt, Satan is operating in a lively way in the atmosphere as well as in the "high places" of men's affairs—governmental, religious, financial, etc. However, it is safe to assume that his throne is in the depths of darkness.

As Satan engaged in spiritual warfare against God's heaven and man's domain, there came One who arose and thundered in victory into the very stronghold of Satan's empire to claim the souls of the righteous dead from their place of rest and transport them to the Presence of God. *"...When he ascended up on high, he led captivity captive..."* (Ephesians 4:8). As He did so, He left His footprint on Satan's face as a seal and promise that one day He will bring the wicked one under complete dominion and wipe out his influence forever.

Genesis 3:15 And I will put enmity between thee and the woman, and between thy seed and her seed; it shall bruise thy head, and thou shalt bruise his heel.

Hebrews 10:13 From henceforth expecting till his enemies be made his footstool.

That time has not yet come, however, and so Satan's evil workings continue in the affairs of men and nations today. How he operates even in the lives of righteous people is an area of great misunderstanding.

Chapter Nine
THE FATHER'S GLORY

The Father's Glory comes to us even we don't deserve it. Why is this? It comes from love.

Prior to the coming of Jesus, the concept of knowing God as a personal Father was virtually unknown to mankind. When the disciples asked Jesus to teach them how to pray, He told them to pray to their Father in Heaven. Envisioning the Creator as a loving Father creates a beautiful picture, full of warmth and intimacy.

Unfortunately, many people, even new believers who are entering the Church, find that the image of God as Father leaves them cold. That's because so many people these days are products of homes broken by divorce or abandonment, where earthly fathers were absent or forced by court order to remain part-time parents at best. For these individuals, the word *father* does not stir up happy thoughts of love and security, but painful memories of rejection, abuse, anger, fear, or loss. Nevertheless, this problem does not set aside the words of the Lord, but rather, puts them in sharp relief.

Everywhere we go, we meet believers and non-believers who long to know the heavenly Father's love. More and more people are coming to Christ while still bearing deep emotional and spiritual wounds. Likewise, we are seeing an increase in supernatural encounters, as our loving God moves to meet the needs of His children. Some of the most glorious testimonies confirm that God's miraculous power occurred as He moved to reveal His "Father's heart" to brokenhearted, wounded people. Like many of you, I, too, have needed healing from a deep "father wound." Let me briefly share some of my journey with you.

Many of us face different obstacles in our pathway that need to be identified and removed so our pipeline to Heaven can be clear and clean. The Lord wants us whole and free, able to receive and respond to His love and revelatory ways. How does this occur? First, we must understand our Father's compassionate nature.

The New Testament is filled with evidence of God's overwhelming love and compassion for us. The truth is that the English word *compassion* doesn't even begin to express the full depth of

God's love, yearning, and brokenness on our behalf. The only way to understand how passionately our Father and His Son care about us is to look at His Word and the language used in it. Jesus had so much compassion for a widow who lost her only son that He stopped the funeral procession and raised him from the dead (see Luke 7:12-15).

Jesus was so brokenhearted over Jerusalem's obstinate ways that He wept over that city, because He knew of the ruin that would come upon it years after His death and resurrection. He said of her people, "How often I wanted to gather your children together, just as a hen gathers her brood under her wings, and you would not have it!" (Luke 13:34b)

The Book of Matthew tells us that when Jesus saw all the people flocking to Him who needed the gospel as well as healing from all sorts of diseases, "**He felt compassion for them, because they were distressed and dispirited like sheep without a shepherd**" (Matt. 9:36). The Book of Mark makes the same statement and indicates that compassion prompted Jesus to feed 5,000 people with only five loaves of bread and two fish, just so they would not have to go away hungry. In a similar situation later on, Jesus saw 4,000 hungry people before Him and said, "I feel compassion for the people because they have remained with Me now three days and have nothing to eat. If I send them away hungry to their homes, they will faint on the way; and some of them have come from a great distance" (Mark 8:2-3). As Jesus' own example demonstrates, compassion always seeks practical expression. Jesus gave us a picture of His Father's compassionate love when He taught His disciples about prayer:

Luke 11:10-13 For every one that asketh receiveth; and he that seeketh findeth; and to him that knocketh it shall be opened. If a son shall ask bread of any of you that is a father, will he give him a stone? or if *he ask* a fish, will he for a fish give him a serpent? Or if he shall ask an egg, will he offer him a scorpion? If ye then, being evil, know how to give good gifts unto your children: how much more shall *your* heavenly Father give the Holy Spirit to them that ask him?

God wants to give us good gifts today, and the first and best gift of all is His Fatherly love. Our first step in receiving this gift is to recognize our Father's compassion toward us and how He wants us to share it with others. Psalm 145:9 (NIV) says, "The Lord is good to all; He has compassion on all He has made." The Psalms also tell us, "But Thou, O Lord, art a God full of compassion, and gracious, longsuffering, and plenteous in mercy and truth" (Ps. 86:15 KJV).

When Jesus shared the story of the prodigal son in Luke 15, He was undoubtedly thinking of His own Father's compassion for His lost, wayward children on earth. You and I are the prodigals in this tale, and God Himself is the loving Father who runs to meet us with great joy. In the parable of the Good Samaritan in Luke 10, we see God's plan to share His love with others in practical and compassionate ways. Every believer is to take for his own the calling of Jesus Christ in Isaiah 61:1-6, which Jesus quoted in Luke 4:18-19 at the launch of His public ministry:

Isaiah 61:1-6 The Spirit of the Lord GOD *is* upon me; because the LORD hath anointed me to preach good tidings unto the meek; he hath sent me to bind up the brokenhearted, to proclaim liberty to the captives, and the opening of the prison to *them that are* bound; To proclaim the acceptable year of the LORD, and the day of vengeance of our God; to comfort all that mourn; To appoint unto them that mourn in Zion, to give unto them beauty for ashes, the oil of joy for mourning, the garment of praise for the spirit of heaviness; that they might be called trees of righteousness, the planting of the LORD, that he might be glorified. And they shall build the old wastes, they shall raise up the former desolations, and they shall repair the waste cities, the desolations of many generations. And strangers shall stand and feed your flocks, and the sons of the alien *shall be* your plowmen and your vinedressers. But ye shall be named the Priests of the LORD: *men* shall call you the Ministers of our God: ye shall eat the riches of the Gentiles, and in their glory shall ye boast yourselves.

The Book of Hebrews tells us that the main reason Jesus is qualified to be our great High Priest is because He was "touched with the feeling of our infirmities" (Heb. 4:15 KJV)

God has made us kings and priests as well, but the only way we can express and share our Father's love with others is to first experience it ourselves.

What is wonderful about God is that even as He trains and commissions us to carry His healing to others, He is healing us! We are asked in the Book of Proverbs, "The spirit of a man will sustain his infirmity; but a wounded spirit who can bear?" (Prov. 18:14 KJV) The New American Standard version states that verse as: "The spirit of a man can endure his sickness, but a broken spirit who can bear?"

Many people don't realize that we are "triune" or three-part beings, much like our Creator is. Man is an eternal spirit who has a soul and dwells in a physical body. Wounds and pain can come to any one of these areas. When we receive Christ as Lord and Savior, our spirit man is instantly, totally transformed into a new being in Christ. Our souls and bodies, however, must be retrained and reformed more slowly over our lifetimes. This explains why it is possible for Christians to be sad, hurt, depressed, or angry.

Here are three basic truths important to understanding the healing process:

1. People have problems that sometimes remain untouched by conversion, the baptism of the Holy Spirit, Bible study, and their own personal prayer and devotional life.

2. Hidden in the recesses of the subconscious mind are hurts and wounds surrounded by feelings that still adversely affect the person's present life.

3. The focus of healing of past hurts is to release hurtful memories so that they no longer negatively affect the individual's present and future. Such release is accomplished primarily through the act of forgiveness.

Hidden hurts that remain even after we are converted to Christ are inflicted upon us by living in a fallen, imperfect world. Wounding also comes through others and sins of the forefathers.

Know that the Lord is greater than of all that, but godly wisdom and knowledge are needed to achieve true freedom. Sounds to me like most of us could use a Father encounter!

We are all subject to the effects of four categories common to life in a fallen world: incidents of history; accidents of nature; disease; and poverty. One or more of these factors affected every major character in the Bible, including God's only begotten Son. What's wonderful is that they all overcame their afflictions to obtain a good report in God.

Jesus had to deal with incidents of history: His earthly father, Joseph, heeded an angel's warning and fled to Egypt to protect Jesus from a vengeful and jealous king. Our Lord also had to deal with political ambitions of the jealous Sadducees and Pharisees, as well as with the racial prejudices of His day.

Any one of us may be carrying hidden wounds that we suffered at the hands of others. These may stem from broken relationships, the work of demonic forces, or sin in our bloodline. Some suffer because of others criminal behavior (such as sexual abuse, rape, or physical abuse), or even prenatal rejections. Many get wounded from entering the world with a false belief of having to prove oneself to earn love and respect, or because parents forced unrealistic and demanding expectations on them. Nearly everyone admits to having pain from wrong choices or for failing to accept personal responsibility in certain areas. This, in turn, can lead to self-destructive bitterness, self-hate, and false expectations.

It's true that we are a product of our decisions. Choices made in the past affect the present and help to make us who we are. What happens in life, however, is not as important as how we respond. We sometimes have little control over what hap-pens, but we can always control our responses. Too often, we get upset and fixated over what we cannot control, instead of focusing on what we can control. When that happens, we react impulsively, fly off the handle, and end up making the situation worse. A careful, considered response often makes the difference between a situation controlling us or our breaking its hold.

God's Word and His eternal laws provide an anchor of stability in the midst of our confusing world. Scripture can help us know how to respond to circumstances of life, whether good or bad. Some of God's laws are eternal and will affect our entire lives, as depending on whether they are broken or honored. Such laws include that of retribution, like the commandment to honor our father and mother, which brings long life on the earth (see Deut. 5:16). Other crucial, divine laws are: Avoid judging others and thus avoid judgment ourselves (see Matt. 7:1-2); and remember that we reap what we sow (see Matt. 7:17; 13:1-23; Gal. 6:7). Of course, there is also the command to never hold others in bondage through unforgiveness (see Matt. 18:21-35).

God's laws of healing include His promises concerning giving and receiving mercy, in that we receive in equal measure to what we give (see Luke 6:36-38). Also of importance is confession and repentance of sin because forgiveness and cleansing come through confession (see 1 John 1:8-9), and ministering forgiveness to one another since healing comes with confession and forgiveness (see John 20:23; James 5:16).

In His parable of the unforgiving servant, Jesus made it clear that we must learn to forgive others unconditionally, no matter what the circumstance (see Matt. 18:15 35; 5:23-24). We must be quick to forgive, no matter who is in the wrong or how badly we hurt. Just as God has forgiven us (see Eph. 4:32), we too must learn to forgive and forget. Forgiveness is God's chief and greatest remedy for what ails us! The reason we must forgive is because unforgiveness always comes back at us. Unforgiveness and bitterness can be traced to almost every disease and life-shortening plague of the human experience. Although not the cause of all diseases, unforgiveness can and does manifest itself through them all. Also, forgiveness can almost always boost the body's ability to fight disease, fatigue, and the effects of life's struggles. Unforgiveness is satan's greatest tool to bring torment and misery to the human race! Remember, we determine our progress by how we respond to circumstances in this life. Unforgiveness gives keys to the devil to unlock his dark slaves and wreak havoc. Don't give the devil the key to your life!

The Bible is filled with examples of how wrong decisions, sin, and failure affected people's lives, and of how God's love and provision still brought victory despite the odds. The daughter of King Saul who was the first wife of King David, adopted a judgmental attitude toward her husband. Her attitude was affected by her father's sin, which caused his demotion from the throne and led to David's being anointed as successor. However, she chose to despise David for his unrestrained worship and praise of God in public. As a result of her sin, she remained barren for the rest of her life (see 2 Sam. 6).

David's sin of adultery with Bathsheba led to serious consequences that brought both immediate sorrow and lasting pain. First, David and Bathsheba suffered the death of their illegitimate child. From then on, the shadow of sexual excess and violence would strike his household repeatedly (see 2 Sam. 12:18). David's son Amnon fell in love with his own half-sister, Tamar, and then raped her. Another son, Absalom, murdered Amnon (his half-brother) to avenge the rape of Tamar. Absalom ultimately rebelled against his own father, King David, and publicly committed adultery with David's concubines in fulfillment of prophecy (see 2 Sam. 16:22). Then Solomon, David's son and successor as king, had his turn. After an illustrious, unprecedented reign of glory and splendor, Solomon fell in his later years because of an unrestrained sexual desire for ungodly women, despite having an unequaled deposit of God's wisdom (see 1 Kings 11:1-8). Solomon's failure sowed the bitter seeds of a divided kingdom, which occurred shortly after his death.

The Book of Genesis describes the many adversities that Joseph the dreamer faced. As the youngest and favored son of Israel (formerly called Jacob), Joseph made his brothers jealous through unwise communication of God's spiritual revelations about his future. His enraged brethren sold Joseph into slavery. But he dealt with this tragic betrayal by forgiving his brothers, and thus escaped the dangers of bitterness. When he finally met his brothers again 20 years later, Joseph wept, which brought further healing through healthy emotional release. Joseph was also able to reinterpret his hurtful experience in the light of God's purposes, and thus freed himself of any negative effects from his bad memories (see Gen.

45:7-8).

Joseph's bad experiences with Potiphar's wife and his subsequent imprisonment did not seem to affect him much! He seemed to forgive easily because he viewed these circumstances in the light of God's plan. Indeed, the Bible repeatedly says, "The Lord was with him" (see Gen. 39:2, 20-23). Joseph kept an eternal perspective, and this point of view helped him choose the proper response. Had he reacted impulsively, rashly, or in anger, his life might well have ended in disaster. Instead, by responding wisely and in faith, Joseph rose from slave to prime minister of Egypt in one day! (See Genesis 41:1-45.) How often might we have robbed ourselves of a blessing because we reacted rashly to a negative situation rather than responding calmly and wisely?

In Luke 24, the two disciples who encountered the resurrected Christ on the road to Emmaus were trying to deal with the pain of numbing disappointment and disillusionment. Jesus entered their emotional world by talking with them, listening to their story, and then exposing their memories of failure and frustration to a new and positive light. He showed them how their despondency was caused by a failure to under-stand God's purposes and by a lack of faith in the Scriptures (see Luke 24:25-26). He then used those same Scripture pas-sages to reinterpret their negative experience and bring new power and hope through revelation (see Luke 24:27). The most powerful change of all came when these men experienced a personal revelation of their risen Lord.

Our Father's remedy for our wounds includes a gift, a service, and a command. First, He gave us His Son, Jesus Christ, who came to "heal the brokenhearted" and "set at liberty them that are bruised" (Luke 4:18 KJV). We must acknowledge that Jesus took our pain and carried our sorrows on the cross of Calvary. He has accomplished it all! This is God's gift to us— it's something we can't earn. We must simply receive the gift.

Second, He provided us with the Holy Spirit, whom Jesus called the "finger of God" (Luke 11:20). One of the Holy Spirit's roles is to reveal the mind of God to us and to point out any hidden bitterness, hurts, wounds, or rejection. God, the Holy Spirit, knows all things, and through His inner work we are conformed to the image of Jesus Christ. The Holy Spirit is the One who will guide us to all truth (see John 16:13). Before a cure can be pronounced, we must allow the Great Physician, in the form of the Holy Spirit, to diagnose our problem. Let Him service His Body and point out specifics in detail.

Third, forgiveness is one of the most important ingredients

for healing and health in our spirits, souls, and bodies. I tell people that God's great remedy for wounded spirits consists of three words: forgive, forgive, forgive! It may be ironic, but it is definitely true: The person who suffers most from unforgiveness is not the unforgiven one, but the person who does not forgive. Likewise, the person who forgives receives a greater blessing than does the one who is forgiven. God issues a command to all of us: Forgive!

Forgiveness involves recognizing that we have been totally forgiven by God, even though we don't deserve it. We must also release any person from the "debt" we feel he or she owes for offending or hurting us. Finally, we must accept the person who offended us for who he or she is. This means releasing the other individual from the responsibility of having to meet our needs in any way. We must forgive, forget, and get on with our life in Christ.

Of course, some specialized situations require more specific ministry. These involve people being affected by the power of inherited spiritual family conditions, such as chronic alcoholism, sexual perversion, child molestation, and other types of social and emotional abuse. Such negative spiritual influences must be renounced and broken in the name of Jesus, and then the truth of God's Word is to be ministered under the Holy Spirit's guidance. In other situations, ungodly "soul ties" or emotional dependencies have a negative impact on a believer's life. These co-dependencies must also be renounced and bro-ken in the name of Jesus. In all these cases, additional Bible teaching—along with compassionate counseling, deliverance ministry, and support from a caring group of people—help these especially troubled believers begin new lives free of oppression through the Holy Spirit's power.

By far, the most prevalent cause of broken hearts and spiritual wounds is rejection. My personal history was laden with these marks, but our Father has shown Himself good to me over many years. Rejection is a sense of being unloved or unwanted by those from whom we want and need love and acceptance the most; rejection is the feeling of being excluded, no matter how much we want to be a part of the group, and of somehow always being on the outside looking in. I once read that one out of every five people in the U.S. has been affected by rejection. Depending on how we define "affected," I believe that we could raise the figure to one out of one!

People suffering from rejection often come from a single-parent family where one parent left or was separated from the family through divorce. Many marriages are dysfunctional in nature, which results in scars on the offspring. These children often admit to suffering from chronic loneliness or depression, and some even advance to various stages of rebellion with its bad fruit and self-destructive behavior. Just as I did, many make negative proclamations about themselves: "I wish I was dead," or "I hate myself." An alarming number of these people either have thought seriously of committing suicide or actually have attempted to do so. Patience, kindness, and great love are needed here. The opposite of rejection is acceptance, and that is exactly what our Father offers each of us through His Son, Jesus Christ.

Regardless of how rejection begins—through illegitimate birth, poverty, parental rejection, family problems, unfair comparisons with others, or self-rejection due to physical characteristics—the results tend to follow predictable patterns. Unfortunately, for every negative emotion, reaction, and attitude, there can be a corresponding demonic spirit. Most people tend to react to rejection internally, where no one can see it; others respond in ways that anyone can see. Whichever the case, the remedies are basically the same: We must submit all patterns of darkness to God's light. Internal reactions to rejection include increased loneliness, self-pity, depression, moodiness, outright despair, despondency, and a sense of hopelessness. These mental strongholds eventually result in death wishes and persistent thoughts of suicide. Such thoughts are particularly dangerous because they are often hidden from the eyes of friends or family who, if they knew, would be willing and able to help.

In every one of these situations, "the way of the Cross leads home." No one suffered more rejection than Jesus, yet He forgave all mankind for that rejection and mistreatment. Even His own Father in Heaven rejected Him as a necessary part of the divine plan for mankind's redemption (see Matt. 27:46; Hab. 1:3). Jesus didn't die from His wounds or the brutality of His crucifixion; He died of a broken heart. His heart had to be broken for us to be healed! In summary, let's review a few pointers in receiving our Father's love and His healing grace.

1. Turn on the Spirit of God. Let the Lord specifically point out the bitterness, hurts, wounds, and rejections that may be hidden in your life. Don't try to conjure it up; let Him bring it to your remembrance.

2. Forgive! Specifically forgive the person or persons who caused that hurt. Remember, forgiveness is an act of your will. It releases people from the debt they "owe" you for the offense, accepts them as they are, and relieves them of responsibility for meeting your needs.

3.	Repent from your own anger or bitterness. Take personal responsibility for your reactions and repent. Then forgive yourself and release God to work in your life.

Our salvation and deliverance from rejection are found in the love of Jesus. Papa God doesn't merely "tolerate" us; He fully accepts us and He always has time for us. We must lay down all bitterness and unforgiveness toward others and give all our hurts to Him. Once we receive the joy and acceptance offered through Jesus, then we will able to walk in supernatural power to set others free. At that point, we can begin to receive and respond to these God encounters. Let the healing come, and may close encounters with the Father's love begin!

Embrace the Papa God who loves you, and let Him fill you with a sense of love and acceptance that you have never known before. If there was a "Father encounter" that awaited me, then there is definitely one for you as well.

Chapter Ten
THE INVISIBLE WAR FOR YOUR MIND

We all have to admit that one of the biggest battles is in the mind. In the invisible, spiritual war for our mind, we will see how the spirit of fear leads us directly into unbelief. Unbelief prevents the promises of God from being received in your life. By studying Satan's operations, we can see that all fear is based on his success in planting seeds of deception in our mind (particularly in our imagination) and getting us to act on them.

In the Church today we hear so much about faith and living the life of faith. Do you know why most people can't exercise true faith? Because they don't have their mind and their imagination under control.

The Bible says that, *"faith is the substance of things hoped for, the evidence of things not seen"* (Hebrews 11:1). When you hope for something, you know exactly what you are hoping for because you picture it in your mind. What you visualize actually shapes what you will become (see Proverbs 23:7). Therefore, faith is the manifestation (or the evidence) of whatever mental pictures you build up in your mind.

Yet many of you are living in such a state of defeat in your minds that you can't imagine that you really are the overcomer that God says you are! You can't imagine that you have total victory over the fears within you. You can't even imagine how you would act if you were fearless.

You do not have the mental picture of yourself that God wants you to have, based on His Word. Instead of seeing yourself as a new person in Christ (fully trusting Him to empower you to overcome), you see only the negative things that dominated your old nature. You are possessed with the past. In your mind's eye you see a whole life of failures based on fears—fears that keep cropping up in your imagination as you yield to them and feed on them.

I don't believe there's a person reading this book who hasn't been attacked by fear in their imagination. For example, from earliest childhood we are programmed by the devil to expect (see ourselves in) poor health in our old age. In our imagination we just know that we will end up with arthritis. We expect our joints to tighten up, our mind to get dull, and our hearing to go bad.

People are constantly telling me, "This illness runs in my family. My father had this pain all his life, and now I've got it. I always knew I'd get it." Where do they get such vain imaginations? Not from the Spirit of God! They are all fueled by fear.

This is why the Spirit of God specifically told Paul that we must rise up and cast down every vain, foul imagination that comes against us (see 2 Corinthians 10:5). Our imagination is the first stronghold that we must bring under control if we are to thoroughly conquer fear.

Did you know that most people who commit adultery picture it first? Sin first comes as a thought in our imagination. It is the same with fear. Fear first comes as a thought from the enemy. If we refuse to rebuke it, then suddenly we're ruled by it. To illustrate this, let's look at a typical example of how this is working in the Church.

Imagine that you have joined a new fellowship and are eager to begin its Wednesday night Bible studies. When that first Wednesday night rolls around, it's cold and rainy outside. The spirit of fear taunts your mind and says, you'd better not go out tonight. The weather is miserable, and you're going to get sick.

You accept this thought and help it along in your imagination. *That's right,* you say to yourself. *I always get sick if I go out when it's like this. If I get a cold this time, I know I'll get pneumonia. I'd better play it safe and stay home just this once.*

So you act on the enemy's seed of fear and stay home. Granted, you do not get a cold, but something dangerous and deceptive has happened. You are now convinced that you remained healthy not because God protected you, but because you stayed home out of the rain!

The next Wednesday night is also chilly and rainy, so you stay home again, unfruitful for God because you're locked into the fear of getting a cold. You have begun to form a habit of obeying the fear instead of obeying God. As the apostle Peter warns us: *"...for of whom a man is overcome, of the same is he brought in bondage"* (2 Peter 2:19).

You have become a slave to fear. Then one day someone tells you that God would be much more pleased if you would act in faith and get out to that Bible study, rain or no rain.

But by now you're even afraid to drive in the rain. Satan has progressed to the next stage of drawing you into bondage, for by now you just can't believe that God would see you through. From this, we can see that all fear is the first step to unbelief.

It is shocking to see how this is exactly the same process which Satan successfully pulled off in the minds of the children of Israel, the same tactics which caused them to fail to enter into the Promised Land of God. Let's see what took place.

In the Book of Numbers, we read how, after years of wandering in the desert, the children of Israel were finally at the gates of the Promised Land. All they had to do was to believe God's Word, trust Him, and enter in. However, they decided to send twelve spies into the territory to check things out first. What happened? Ten out of the twelve spies disobeyed God by taking their eyes off of Him and His promises and putting them on their enemies instead.

Seeing this, Satan immediately went to work on their minds. By the time the ten stood up to give their report to the people, the spirit of fear had total control of their imaginations. Instead of expressing faith in God, they could only rebel in unbelief and wail:

Numbers 13:32, 33 And they brought up an evil report of the land which they had searched unto the children of Israel, saying, The land, through which we have gone to search it, *is* a land that eateth up the inhabitants thereof; and all the people that we saw in it *are* men of a great stature. And there we saw the giants, the sons of Anak, *which come* of the giants: and we were in our own sight as grasshoppers, and so we were in their sight.

From this, we learn a very important lesson. That is, Satan's end objective is not merely to keep you in bondage to fear but to lull you into a state of unbelief through that fear. And unbelief always leads to rebellion against God's Word!

Remember, although Satan had successfully instilled fears in the minds of the children of Israel, God did not ban them from the Promised Land because their imaginations had gone wild. What really hammered the nails into their coffins was the fact that after they had surrendered to fear, *"...they could not enter in because of unbelief"* (Hebrews 3:19).

Right now, I beg you to realize that your "little fears" are far more dangerous in the long run than you may suspect. Ultimately, each one of them will lead to unbelief and a dangerous denial of God and His Word, which is considered (in His eyes) rebellion. Please, I beg you to face this question today: Who has control of my thoughts and my imagination, Satan or God?

Unfortunately, what happened to the children of Israel was no isolated incident. I see Satan's same fear tactics take root in the imaginations of countless Christians day after day. Jesus said, *"...if therefore thine eye be single, thy whole body shall be full of light"* (Matthew 6:22). There is no way that any fear can hover in the dark recesses of your mind when your eye is single-mindedly set on your Lord and His Word. You're afraid today because you have your eyes glued to the wrong place. You are being ruled by what has been.

Think about it. Pinpoint your own fears. When did you first experience them? In childhood? After an auto accident? When your parents were divorced? The first time a door was slammed in your face? Whatever it was, that incident (or incidents) was a point of entry for Satan to plant seeds of guilt and fear in your old nature, and you got stuck there. You began to talk yourself into believing that all of the pain and fears of the past were still real. You kept them alive through your self-talk.

Make no mistake. Words are powerful. Even the silent words that you "speak" in conversations with yourself have a dramatic effect on your entire being. Through your self-talk you can literally talk yourself into cooperating with the spirit of fear, and remain in bondage to it. "If I get close to anybody, they'll only use me, so I'd better keep my distance," you say. So, you never get close to anyone, not even God.

"I'll never get married. I can't stand all of the fighting."

"I hate religion. When I was a kid, my folks dragged me to church. I'll never go again."

"I'll never be able to give. We've always been poor."

What you are really saying through all of this is, "I really don't believe I'm a new creation in Christ Jesus. I'm afraid to let go. I'm afraid to fully surrender myself to the Lord. I'm afraid to trust Him to remold my life. I'll just stay the way I am."

Stop telling yourself these things! The Word of God is commanding you:

Isaiah 43:18, 19 Remember ye not the former things, neither consider the things of old. Behold, I will do a new thing; now it shall spring forth; shall ye not know it? I will even make a way in the wilderness, *and* rivers in the desert.

When God first informed Jeremiah that he was called to be a prophet, the boy's first reaction was fear. *"...Ah, Lord God! behold, I cannot speak: for I am a child"* (Jeremiah 1:6). God immediately admonished him:

Jeremiah 1:7, 8 But the LORD said unto me, Say not, I *am* a child: for thou shalt go to all that I shall send thee, and whatsoever I command thee thou shalt speak. Be not afraid of their faces: for I *am* with thee to deliver thee, saith the LORD.

Jeremiah 1:17, 18 Thou therefore gird up thy loins, and arise, and speak unto them all that I command thee: be not dismayed at their faces, lest I confound thee before them. For, behold, I have made thee this day a defenced city, and an iron pillar, and brasen walls against the whole land, against the kings of Judah, against the princes thereof, against the priests thereof, and against the people of the land.

Notice that the first thing God corrected with Jeremiah was his self-talk, telling him, Then He went after the image that Jeremiah had of himself, changing it from the fearful one that Jeremiah had clung to (based on what he was in the past), to the one that God was shaping for him in the present. God had great things in store for Jeremiah, but Jeremiah had to face his fears and get rid of his past image first, starting with his thoughts and the way he talked to himself.

Right now the Word of God promises you that, *"whatsoever thou shalt bind on earth shall be bound in heaven"* (Matthew 16:19). This includes all of those poisonous thoughts that fuel the spirit of fear! As of today, start binding and casting out those demonically-inspired thoughts from your mind. Today is a new day. You are a new creation, and God is commanding you:

Ephesians 4:22-24 That ye put off concerning the former conversation the old man, which is corrupt according to the deceitful lusts; And be renewed in the spirit of your mind; And that ye put on the new man, which after God is created in righteousness and true holiness.

Believe me, God would not command you to do something if you could not do it.

The Spirit of God is telling you: *"Fear not. Cut the shorelines of your past. A new day is breaking forth upon you. Even now, press through into that which you have spoken unto Me, that which is your heart's desire. Be free from fear. Step out into My love, and you will not sink. You will see My power and My faithfulness in cutting loose those things which have held you in bondage to fear. Release yourself into a new dependence upon Me."*

You are ready to press on past the past. From now on, you're going to be able to draw a line and separate the thoughts of your "old self" of the past from the things the Spirit of God is telling your new self. This does not mean that all of the fears associated with your past will never come up before you again. It does mean that when they do, you are not going to wait five seconds before you successfully deal with them. How?

You are about to enter a new dimension of spiritual strength, a new strength that you have never experienced before. You are about to become an overcomer!

About the Author

Bill Vincent is no stranger to understanding the power of God. Not only has he spent over twenty years as a Minister with a strong prophetic anointing, he is now also an Apostle and Author with Revival Waves of Glory Ministries in Litchfield, IL. Along with his wife, Tabitha, he, leads a team providing apostolic oversight in all aspects of ministry, including service, personal ministry and Godly character.

Bill offers a wide range of writings and teachings from deliverance, to experiencing presence of God and developing Apostolic cutting edge Church structure. Drawing on the power of the Holy Spirit through years of experience in Revival, Spiritual Sensitivity, and deliverance ministry, Bill now focuses mainly on pursuing the Presence of God and breaking the power of the devil off of people's lives.

His books 48 and counting has since helped many people to overcome the spirits and curses of Satan. For more information or to keep up with Bill's latest releases, please visit www.revivalwavesofgloryministries.com. To contact Bill, feel free to follow him on twitter @revivalwaves.

Recommended Books

By Bill Vincent

Overcoming Obstacles

Glory: Pursuing God's Presence

Defeating the Demonic Realm

Increasing Your Prophetic Gift

Increase Your Anointing

Keys to Receiving Your Miracle

The Supernatural Realm

Waves of Revival

Increase of Revelation and Restoration

The Resurrection Power of God

Discerning Your Call of God

Apostolic Breakthrough

Glory: Increasing God's Presence

Love is Waiting – Don't Let Love Pass You By

The Healing Power of God

Glory: Expanding God's Presence

Receiving Personal Prophecy

Signs and Wonders

Signs and Wonders Revelations

Children Stories

The Rapture

The Secret Place of God's Power

Building a Prototype Church

Breakthrough of Spiritual Strongholds

Glory: Revival Presence of God

Overcoming the Power of Lust

Glory: Kingdom Presence of God

Transitioning to the Prototype Church

The Stronghold of Jezebel

Healing After Divorce

A Closer Relationship With God

Cover Up and Save Yourself

Desperate for God's Presence

The War for Spiritual Battles

Spiritual Leadership

Global Warning

Millions of Churches

Destroying the Jezebel Spirit

Awakening of Miracles

Deception and Consequences Revealed

Are You a Follower of Christ

Don't Let the Enemy Steal from You!

A Godly Shaking

The Unsearchable Riches of Christ

Heaven's Court System

Satan's Open Doors

Armed for Battle

The Wrestler

Spiritual Warfare: Complete Collection

Growing In the Prophetic

The Prototype Church: Complete Edition

Faith

The Angry Fighter's Story

Understanding Heaven's Court System

Web Site:

www.revivalwavesofgloryministries.com

www.ingramcontent.com/pod-product-compliance
Lightning Source LLC
Chambersburg PA
CBHW052056070526
44584CB00017B/2214